A TREASURY OF XXth CENTURY MURDER

The Lindbergh Child

cloth: ISBN 10: 1-56163-529-4
ISBN 13: 978-1-56163-529-0
paperback: ISBN 10: 1-56163-530-8
ISBN 13: 978-1-56163-530-6
Printed in China

5   4   3   2   1

Comicslit is an imprint and
trademark of

NANTIER · BEALL · MINOUSTCHINE
Publishing inc.
new york

THE LINDBERGH CHILD

THE
SENSATIONAL
CASE THAT
TRANSFIXED
THE NATION.

THE
QUESTIONS
THAT REMAIN
TO THIS
DAY.

THE ATROCIOUS KIDNAPPING
AND MURDER OF THE INFANT SON
OF AMERICA'S HERO
Col. CHARLES A. LINDBERGH

THE HOUSE AT
HOPEWELL, NEW JERSEY

WRITTEN AND ILLUSTRATED by
RICK GEARY

NBM
ComicsLit

A Treasury of Victorian Murder
Jack the Ripper
Rick Geary

A TREASURY OF VICTORIAN MURDER
The Borden Tragedy
Rick Geary

The Fatal Bullet
The Assassination of President James A. Garfield
RICK GEARY

The Mystery of Mary Rogers
Rick Geary

A TREASURY OF VICTORIAN MURDER
The Beast of Chicago
The Murderous Career of H. H. Holmes
RICK GEARY

The Murder of Abraham Lincoln
RICK GEARY

The Case of Madeleine Smith
RICK GEARY

The Saga of the Bloody Benders
RICK GEARY

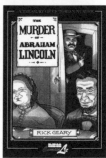

THE LINDBERGH CHILD

BIBLIOGRAPHY

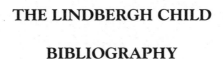

Behn, Noel, *Lindbergh: The Crime.* (New York, Atlantic Monthly Press, 1994)

Douglas, John and Mark Olshaker, *The Cases That Haunt Us.* (New York, Scribner, 2000)

Fisher, Jim, *The Ghosts of Hopewell, Setting the Record Straight in the Lindbergh Case.* (Carbondale IL, Southern Illinois University Press, 1999)

Linbergh, Anne Morrow, *Hour of Gold, Hour of Lead.* (New York, Signet Books, 1974)

Mappen, Marc, *Murder and Spies, Lovers and Lies: Settling the Great Controversies of American History.* (New York, Avon Books, 1996)

Waller, George, *Kidnap: The Story of the Linbergh Case.* (New York, The Dial Press, 1961)

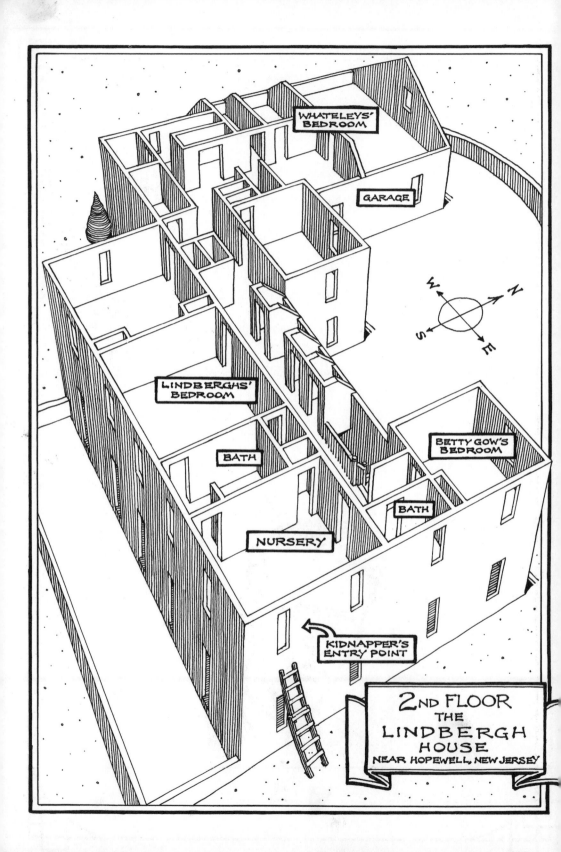

WHATELEYS' BEDROOM

GARAGE

W N S E

LINDBERGHS' BEDROOM

BETTY GOW'S BEDROOM

BATH

BATH

NURSERY

KIDNAPPER'S ENTRY POINT

2ND FLOOR
THE
LINDBERGH
HOUSE
NEAR HOPEWELL, NEW JERSEY

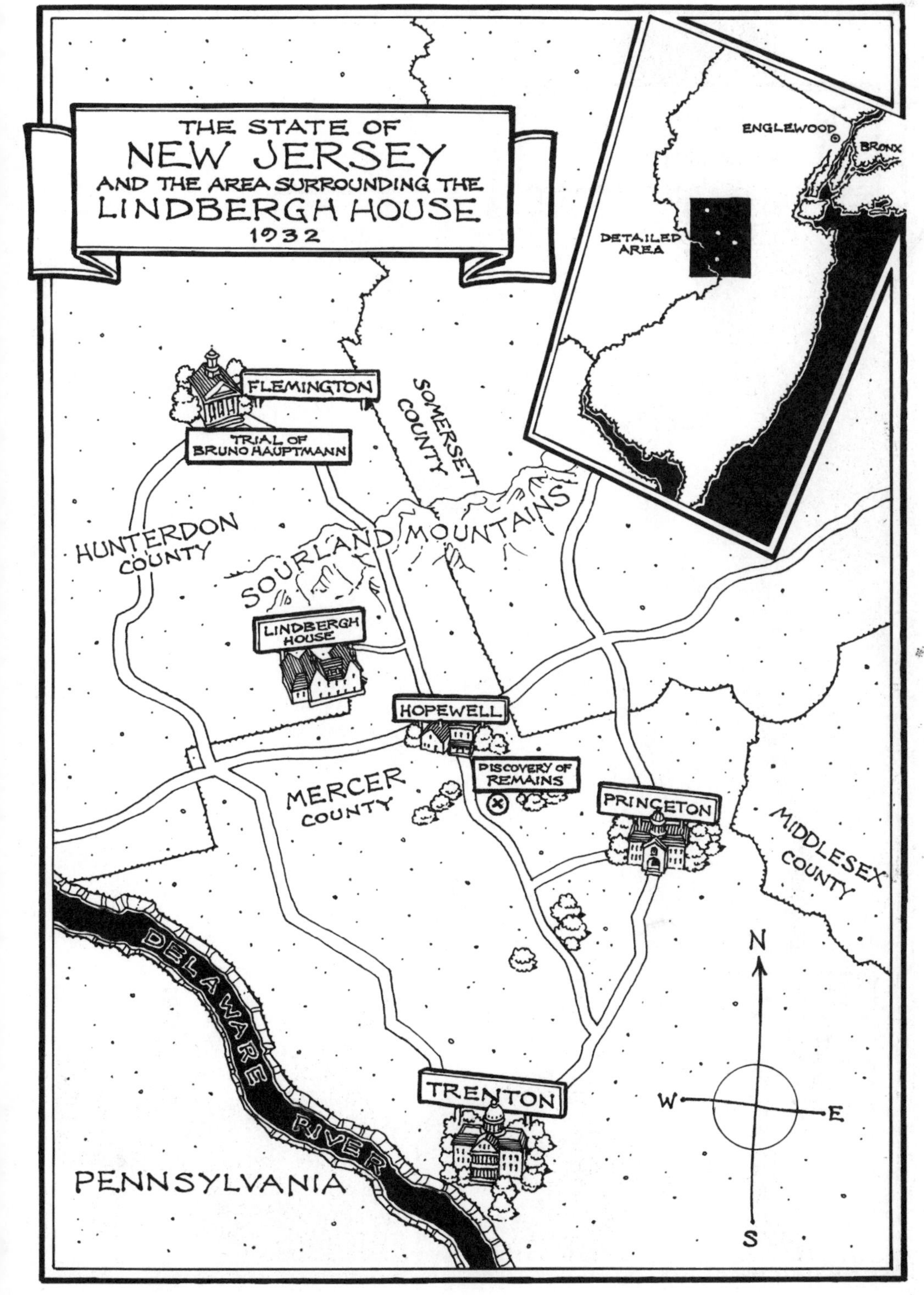
THE STATE OF
NEW JERSEY
AND THE AREA SURROUNDING THE
LINDBERGH HOUSE
1932
ENGLEWOOD
BRONX
DETAILED AREA
FLEMINGTON
TRIAL OF BRUNO HAUPTMANN
SOMERSET COUNTY
SOURLAND MOUNTAINS
HUNTERDON COUNTY
LINDBERGH HOUSE
HOPEWELL
DISCOVERY OF REMAINS
MERCER COUNTY
PRINCETON
MIDDLESEX COUNTY
DELAWARE RIVER
TRENTON
PENNSYLVANIA
N
W
E
S

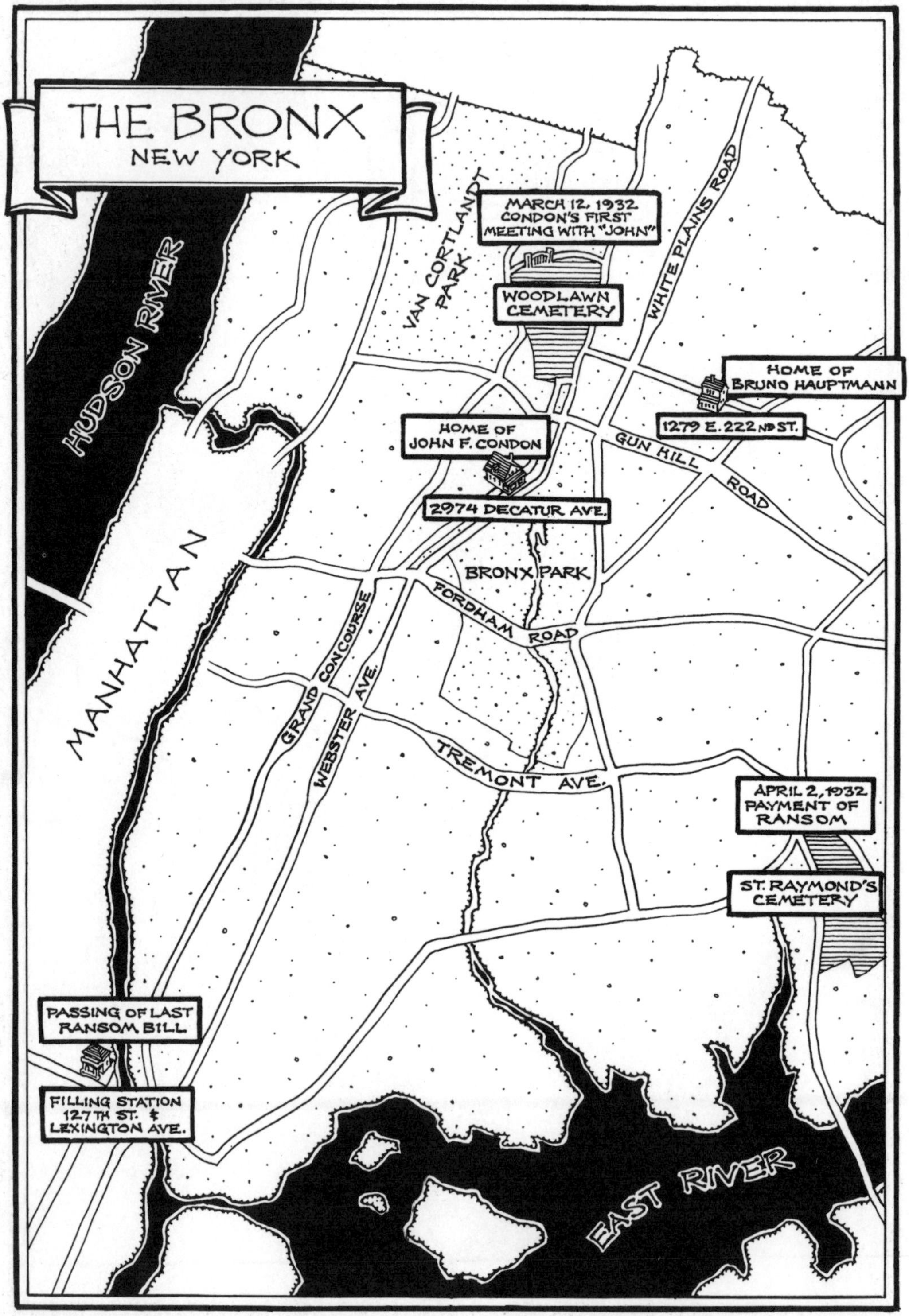
THE BRONX
NEW YORK
HUDSON RIVER
VAN CORTLANDT PARK
MARCH 12, 1932
CONDON'S FIRST
MEETING WITH "JOHN"
WOODLAWN
CEMETERY
WHITE PLAINS ROAD
HOME OF
BRUNO HAUPTMANN
1279 E. 222ND ST.
HOME OF
JOHN F. CONDON
2974 DECATUR AVE.
GUN HILL ROAD
MANHATTAN
BRONX PARK
FORDHAM ROAD
GRAND CONCOURSE
WEBSTER AVE.
TREMONT AVE.
APRIL 2, 1932
PAYMENT OF
RANSOM
ST. RAYMOND'S
CEMETERY
PASSING OF LAST
RANSOM BILL
FILLING STATION
127TH ST. &
LEXINGTON AVE.
EAST RIVER

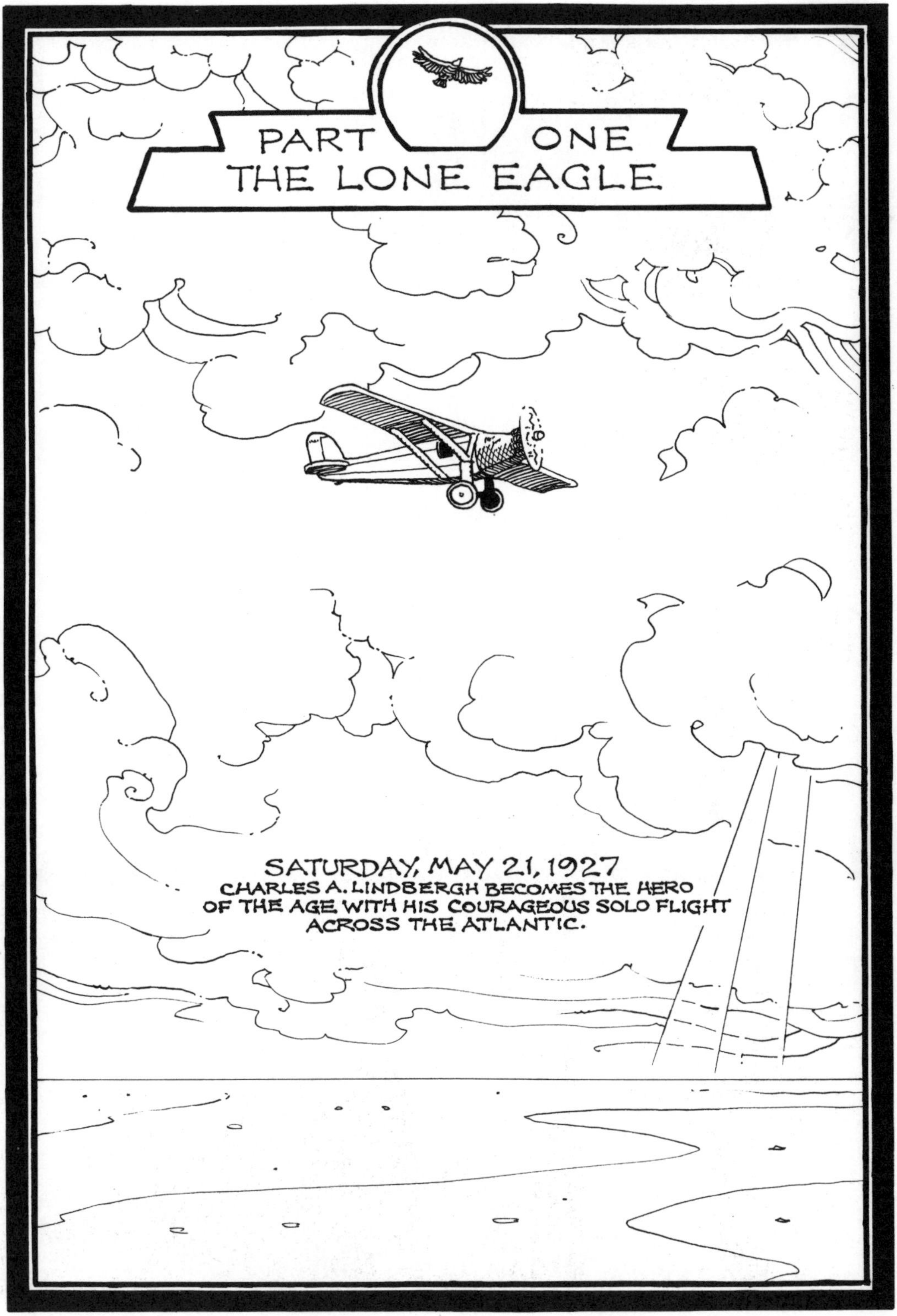
PART ONE
THE LONE EAGLE
SATURDAY, MAY 21, 1927
CHARLES A. LINDBERGH BECOMES THE HERO OF THE AGE WITH HIS COURAGEOUS SOLO FLIGHT ACROSS THE ATLANTIC.

AFTER 33½ HOURS IN THE AIR, HE LANDS HIS TINY PLANE AT LE BOURGET FIELD IN PARIS.

TUMULT! ECSTASY! INTERNATIONAL ADULATION!

FOUR MILLION PACK THE STREETS OF NEW YORK CITY JUST TO CATCH A GLIMPSE OF HIM.

THE SHY, HANDSOME, 25-YEAR-OLD WEARS HIS FAME WITH GRACE AND MODESTY. INCIDENTALLY, HE IS A BACHELOR.

BUT NOT FOR LONG! WHILE ON A GOOD-WILL MISSION TO MEXICO CITY IN DECEMBER OF 1927, HE STAYS AT THE HOME OF DWIGHT MORROW, THE AMERICAN AMBASSADOR.

HERE HE MEETS AND FALLS IN LOVE WITH ANNE, AGE 21, SECOND-OLDEST OF THE MORROWS' FOUR OFFSPRING.

ELISABETH

ANNE

DWIGHT, JR.

CONSTANCE

ON MAY 27, 1929, THEY MARRY.

THE NEW MRS. LINDBERGH PROVES AS INTREPID AS HER HUSBAND, AS SHE ACCOMPANIES HIM ON HIS AVIATION EXPLOITS.

TOGETHER, THEY SET A TRANSCONTINENTAL SPEED RECORD AND MAP AIR ROUTES TO THE FAR EAST.

ALL THE WHILE, THEY MUST ENDURE THE SCRUTINY OF THE CURIOUS PUBLIC AND THE EVER-INTRUSIVE PRESS.

THE AVIATOR'S CELEBRITY, HOWEVER, IS CRUCIAL TO THE FLEDGELING AIRLINE INDUSTRY, IN WHOSE FUTURE HE BELIEVES FERVENTLY.

THE COUPLE'S DESIRE FOR SECLUSION ONLY INTENSIFIES WHEN, ON JUNE 22, 1930, ANNE GIVES BIRTH TO A SON — CHARLES AUGUSTUS LINDBERGH, JR.

THE PUBLIC HUNGERS FOR THE SMALLEST TIDBIT OF NEWS CONCERNING THE INFANT.

LATER IN THE YEAR, THE LINDBERGHS PURCHASE A TRACT OF 360 ACRES NEAR THE VILLAGE OF HOPEWELL, NEW JERSEY — BELOW THE SOURLAND MOUNTAINS, ABOUT 15 MILES FROM PRINCETON.

HERE, THEY BEGIN CONSTRUCTION ON A LARGE HOUSE — THEIR SANCTUARY.

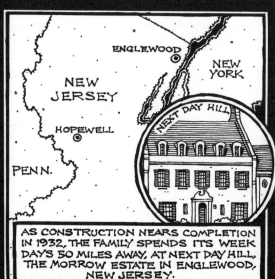

AS CONSTRUCTION NEARS COMPLETION IN 1932, THE FAMILY SPENDS ITS WEEK DAYS 50 MILES AWAY, AT NEXT DAY HILL, THE MORROW ESTATE IN ENGLEWOOD, NEW JERSEY.

ANNE IS AT WORK ON A BOOK OF HER ASIAN TRAVELS, WHILE CHARLES TRAVELS DAILY TO HIS OFFICE IN NEW YORK CITY.

WEEKENDS FIND THEM IN RESIDENCE AT THEIR NEW HOME, THOUGH MUCH OF THE INTERIOR REMAINS UNFINISHED.

THE SOLITUDE OF THEIR LOCATION, THE BLEAK BEAUTY OF THE COUNTRYSIDE, PROVIDE THE PEACE AND RESPITE THEY LONG FOR.

THEIR PERSONAL STAFF CONSISTS OF THREE INDIVIDUALS.

THE ENGLISH BUTLER, ALOYSIUS "OLLY" WHATELEY AND HIS WIFE, ELSIE, WHO SERVES AS COOK AND HOUSEKEEPER.

AND THE BABY'S NURSEMAID, BETTY GOW, AGE 25, A RECENT IMMIGRANT FROM SCOTLAND.

PART TWO
THE CRIME

THE WEEKEND OF FEBRUARY 27-28, 1932,
FINDS THE LINDBERGHS, ACCORDING TO RECENT
CUSTOM, AT THEIR NEW HOME.

DURING THIS TIME, CHARLES, JR. DEVELOPS A
SERIOUS COLD, AND ON MONDAY, FEBRUARY 29,
MRS. LINDBERGH DECIDES NOT TO RETURN TO
ENGLEWOOD.

TUESDAY, MARCH 1, 1932

THE EVENTS OF THIS DAY ARE ATTESTED TO BY COLONEL AND MRS. LINDBERGH AND THEIR SERVANTS.

IN THE MORNING, THE BABY'S COLD NOT HAVING ABATED, ANNE LINDBERGH SUMMONS BETTY GOW, WHO HAS BEEN WAITING AT NEXT DAY HILL.

THE NURSEMAID ARRIVES AT ABOUT 2:00 PM.

BY AFTERNOON, THE CHILD SEEMS SOMEWHAT IMPROVED...

AND AT 6:15 PM, THE TWO WOMEN BEGIN TO PREPARE HIM FOR BED.

THEY DRESS HIM IN HIS WOOLEN DR. DENTON SLEEPING SUIT,...

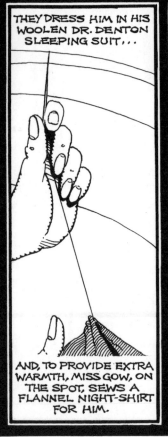

AND, TO PROVIDE EXTRA WARMTH, MISS GOW, ON THE SPOT, SEWS A FLANNEL NIGHT-SHIRT FOR HIM.

TWO WIRE THUMB-GUARDS ARE SECURED TO THE INFANT'S HANDS.

(AT COL. LINDBERGH'S INSISTANCE, AS PREVENTATIVE OF THUMB-SUCKING.)

MRS. LINDBERGH CLOSES THE SHUTTERS OF TWO OF THE ROOM'S THREE WINDOWS.

SHE HAS TROUBLE WITH THE PAIR IN THE SOUTHEAST CORNER. THEY ARE WARPED AND WILL NOT QUITE COME TOGETHER.

SHE LEAVES THE ROOM AT 7:30, AS MISS GOW SECURES THE BABY IN HIS CRIB BY MEANS OF TWO LARGE SAFETY PINS.

THE NURSEMAID REMAINS IN THE ROOM UNTIL SHE IS CERTAIN HER CHARGE IS ASLEEP...

LEAVING AT ABOUT 8:00 PM TO JOIN ELSIE WHATELEY IN THE SERVANT'S SITTING ROOM.

THE EVENING HAS TURNED COLD AND BLUSTERY AS COL. LINDBERGH ARRIVES HOME AT ABOUT 8:30 PM.

AFTER A FULL DAY OF APPOINTMENTS, HE HAS FORGOTTEN AN IMPORTANT ENGAGEMENT THIS EVENING. HE WAS TO BE GUEST OF HONOR AT NEW YORK UNIVERSITY'S ALL-ALUMNI CENTENNIAL DINNER.

TWO THOUSAND ATTENDEES AWAIT HIM AT THE WALDORF-ASTORIA HOTEL.

AS THE LINDBERGHS SIT DOWN TO DINNER, BETTY GOW TALKS ON THE TELEPHONE TO HER BOYFRIEND, HENRY "RED" JOHNSEN.

REGRETABLY, SHE HAS TO BREAK THEIR DATE FOR THIS EVENING.

AFTER DINNER, HUSBAND AND WIFE RELAX IN THE IN THE LIVING ROOM.

AT ONE POINT, THE COLONEL HEARS A NOISE FROM OUTSIDE — A SHARP SOUND LIKE BREAKING WOOD.

NOTHING IS THOUGHT OF THIS, SINCE THE NIGHT IS UNUSUALLY WINDY.

AT 9:30 PM, THE LINDBERGHS CLIMB THE STAIRS TO THEIR BEDROOM.

SHORTLY THEREAFTER, CHARLES RETURNS DOWNSTAIRS TO WORK IN THE LIBRARY...

WHICH IS SITUATED DIRECTLY BELOW THE NURSERY.

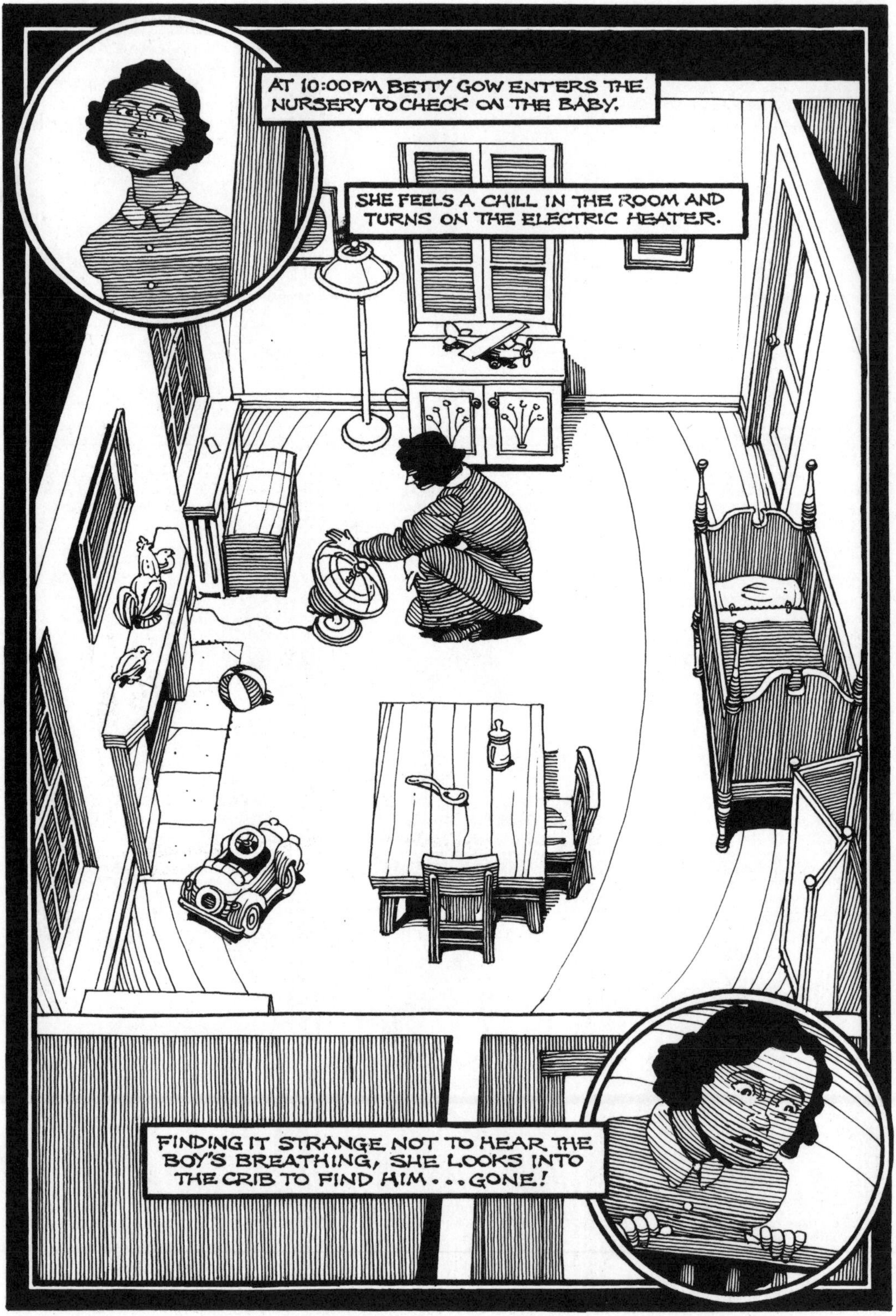
AT 10:00 PM BETTY GOW ENTERS THE NURSERY TO CHECK ON THE BABY.
SHE FEELS A CHILL IN THE ROOM AND TURNS ON THE ELECTRIC HEATER.
FINDING IT STRANGE NOT TO HEAR THE BOY'S BREATHING, SHE LOOKS INTO THE CRIB TO FIND HIM...GONE!

MISS GOW'S FIRST THOUGHT IS THAT THE BOY IS WITH HIS MOTHER. BUT ANNE LINDBERGH WONDERS IF CHARLES TOOK HIM AS A PRACTICAL JOKE, FOR WHICH THE AVIATOR IS NOTORIOUS.

THIS IS QUICKLY FOUND NOT TO BE THE CASE.

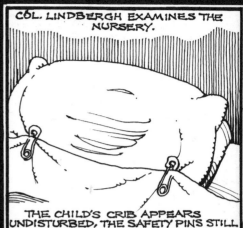

COL. LINDBERGH EXAMINES THE NURSERY.

THE CHILD'S CRIB APPEARS UNDISTURBED, THE SAFETY PINS STILL IN PLACE ON THE BLANKET, THE IMPRINT OF HIS TINY HEAD STILL ON THE PILLOW.

THE SOUTHEAST WINDOW IS CLOSED, BUT NEXT TO IT, ON THE RADIATOR COVER, LIES AN ENVELOPE.

ON THE CHEST BENEATH THE WINDOW CAN BE DISCERNED SMUDGES OF MUD.

HE THINKS IT BEST TO TOUCH NOTHING IN THE ROOM, PENDING THE ARRIVAL OF POLICE.

ANNE, WITH BETTY GOW AND ELSIE WHATELEY, GIVE THE REST OF THE HOUSE A THOROUGH SEARCH.

WHILE COL. LINDBERGH, RIFLE IN HAND, AND OLLY WHATELEY GO OVER THE GROUNDS.

IN QUICK SUCCESSION, THREE TELEPHONE CALLS ARE PLACED...

TO THE MERCER COUNTY SHERIFF'S OFFICE IN HOPEWELL...

TO HENRY BRECKINRIDGE, THE LINDBERGHS' ATTORNEY AND FAMILY FRIEND...

TO THE NEW JERSEY STATE POLICE.

AT ABOUT 10:40PM, THE FIRST SHERIFF DEPUTIES ARRIVE. OUTSIDE THE HOUSE, THEY FIND SEVERAL CLUES.

DIRECTLY BENEATH THE SOUTHEAST NURSERY WINDOW ARE TWO IMPRESSIONS IN THE MUD— APPARENTLY FROM A LADDER.

CLOSE BY IS WHAT LOOKS LIKE A SHOEPRINT.

UPON SCRUTINY, IT REVEALS UNEVEN EDGES AND A TEXTILE PATTERN, AS IF SOCKS OR BURLAP WERE WORN OVER SHOES.

SOME DISTANCE AWAY IS FOUND A THREE-QUARTER-INCH CARPENTER'S CHISEL ...

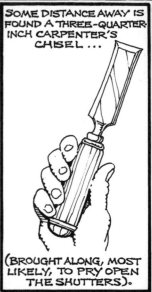

(BROUGHT ALONG, MOST LIKELY, TO PRY OPEN THE SHUTTERS).

A LITTLE FARTHER TO THE SOUTHEAST, WHAT WILL TURN OUT TO BE THE MOST IMPORTANT PIECE OF EVIDENCE: A THREE-PART EXTENSION LADDER, OBVIOUSLY HAND-MADE, LYING IN TWO SECTIONS.

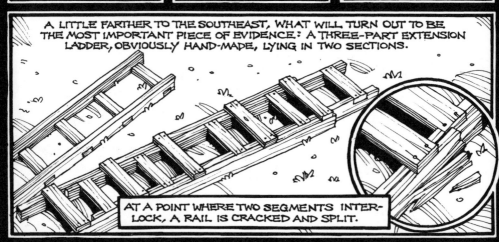

AT A POINT WHERE TWO SEGMENTS INTER-LOCK, A RAIL IS CRACKED AND SPLIT.

TO THE EAST OF THE HOUSE IS A ROUGH ACCESS ROAD CALLED FEATHERBED LANE. COULD THIS HAVE BEEN THE KIDNAPPER'S ROUTE?

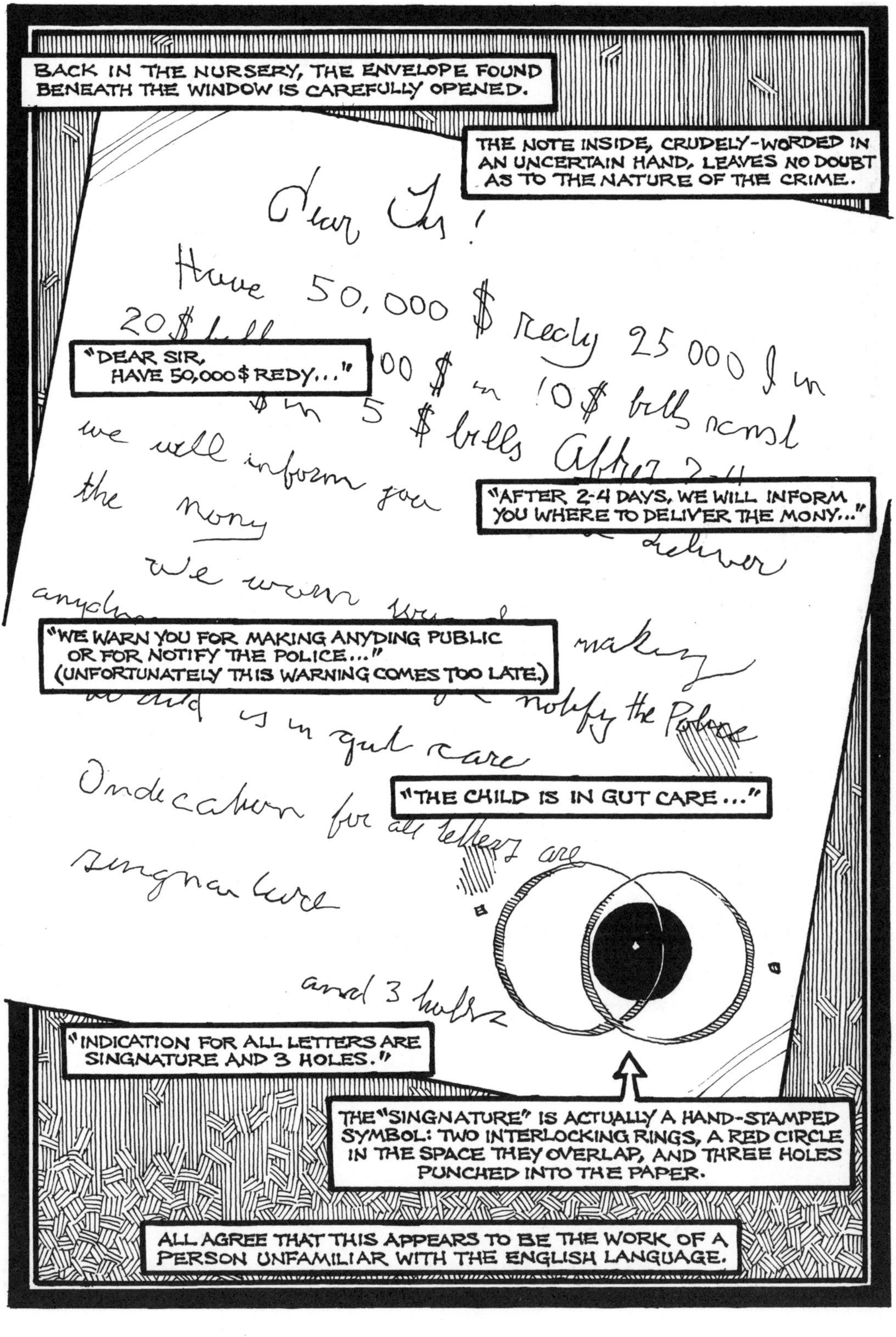

BACK IN THE NURSERY, THE ENVELOPE FOUND BENEATH THE WINDOW IS CAREFULLY OPENED.
THE NOTE INSIDE, CRUDELY-WORDED IN AN UNCERTAIN HAND, LEAVES NO DOUBT AS TO THE NATURE OF THE CRIME.
"DEAR SIR, HAVE 50,000$ REDY..."
"AFTER 2-4 DAYS, WE WILL INFORM YOU WHERE TO DELIVER THE MONY..."
"WE WARN YOU FOR MAKING ANYDING PUBLIC OR FOR NOTIFY THE POLICE..." (UNFORTUNATELY THIS WARNING COMES TOO LATE.)
"THE CHILD IS IN GUT CARE..."
"INDICATION FOR ALL LETTERS ARE SINGNATURE AND 3 HOLES."
THE "SINGNATURE" IS ACTUALLY A HAND-STAMPED SYMBOL: TWO INTERLOCKING RINGS, A RED CIRCLE IN THE SPACE THEY OVERLAP, AND THREE HOLES PUNCHED INTO THE PAPER.
ALL AGREE THAT THIS APPEARS TO BE THE WORK OF A PERSON UNFAMILIAR WITH THE ENGLISH LANGUAGE.

BY 11:00 PM, POLICE HAVE ESTABLISHED STATEWIDE ROADBLOCKS.

ANY CAR CONTAINING A CHILD IS DETAINED FOR QUESTIONING.

RESIDENTS OF THE AREA DESCRIBE HAVING SEEN SUSPICIOUS-LOOKING CARS CARRYING SUSPICIOUS-LOOKING PEOPLE THROUGHOUT THE PREVIOUS DAY.

A MYSTERIOUS GREEN CAR IS MENTIONED BY MORE THAN ONE PERSON.

BY MIDNIGHT, THE AIRWAVES ARE ABUZZ WITH THE NEWS...

AND, THROUGHOUT THE MORNING, THE PRESS DESCENDS UPON TINY HOPEWELL.

WEDNESDAY, MARCH 2 — BY MID-MORNING, THE NEW JERSEY STATE POLICE HAVE SET UP A HEADQUARTERS INSIDE THE LINDBERGHS' GARAGE.

THE INVESTIGATION IS HEADED BY THE STATE POLICE SUPERINTENDENT, COL. H. NORMAN SCHWARZKOPF.

THE JUSTICE DEPARTMENT'S BUREAU OF INVESTIGATION, DIRECTED BY J. EDGAR HOOVER, OFFERS ITS ASSISTANCE...

ALTHOUGH AT THIS TIME, THERE IS LITTLE, BY LAW, THAT IT CAN DO.

BY MID-DAY, THE ROADS INTO HOPEWELL ARE JAMMED.

JOURNALISTS AND THE CURIOUS PUBLIC ROAM FREELY ABOUT THE LINDBERGH PROPERTY...

UNTIL THEY ARE AT LAST CLEARED AWAY BY THE POLICE.

FORENSIC EXAMINERS CAN FIND NO FINGERPRINTS ON THE RANSOM NOTE, THE LADDER, THE CHISEL, OR ANYPLACE IN THE NURSERY—NOT EVEN THOSE OF THE FAMILY.

THIS IS DEEMED STRANGE BY ALL.

COL. LINDBERGH FEELS THAT THE KIDNAPPER'S INSTRUCTIONS MUST BE FOLLOWED FAITHFULLY, AS THE BEST WAY TO GET HIS SON BACK SAFELY.

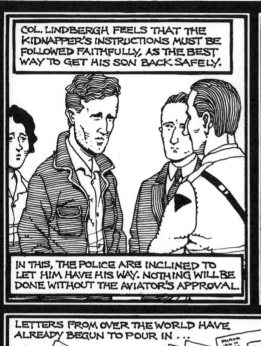

IN THIS, THE POLICE ARE INCLINED TO LET HIM HAVE HIS WAY. NOTHING WILL BE DONE WITHOUT THE AVIATOR'S APPROVAL.

MRS. LINDBERGH MAKES UP A LIST OF THE BABY'S DIET REQUIREMENTS.

A half cup of orange juice or
One quart of milk during the
Three tablespoons of cooked ce
Two tablespoons of cooked ve
The yolk of one egg daily.
One baked potato or rice once a da
Two tablespoons of stewed fruit
A half-cup of prune juice after the
Fourteen drops of viosterol, a vitam
during the day.

IT IS DISTRIBUTED TO EVERY MAJOR NEWSPAPER AND WIRE SERVICE.

LETTERS FROM OVER THE WORLD HAVE ALREADY BEGUN TO POUR IN . . .

OFFERING SYMPATHY, ADVICE, AND ACCUSATION.

THE ASSUMPTION OF LINDBERGH AND BRECKINRIDGE AND SEVERAL OTHERS IS THAT THE CRIME WAS COMMITTED BY A GANG OF PROFESSIONALS.

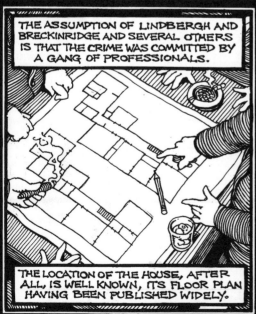

THE LOCATION OF THE HOUSE, AFTER ALL, IS WELL KNOWN, ITS FLOOR PLAN HAVING BEEN PUBLISHED WIDELY.

KIDNAPPING IS LUCRATIVE WORK FOR GANGS DURING THESE DEPRESSION YEARS.

SEVERAL WEALTHY VICTIMS HAVE BEEN RELEASED UNHARMED AFTER PAYMENT OF THE RANSOM.

ANOTHER SCHOOL OF THOUGHT HOLDS THAT IT WAS CARRIED OUT BY A GROUP OF AMATEURS...

PERHAPS WITH THE AID OF A MEMBER OF THE LINDBERGHS' OR MORROWS' STAFF.

OTHERWISE, HOW WOULD THE KIDNAPPERS HAVE KNOWN THAT THE FAMILY HAD VARIED ITS ROUTINE AND STAYED AT HOPEWELL ANOTHER TWO NIGHTS?

WOULDN'T THE CHILD HAVE CRIED OUT IF PICKED UP BY UNFAMILIAR HANDS?

ALSO, THE LINDBERGHS' FOX TERRIER "WAGOOSH," KNOWN FOR BARKING AT THE SMALLEST INTRUSION, WAS STRANGELY SILENT LAST NIGHT.

THE RANSOM NOTE IS "UNPROFESSIONAL": IN A STILTED HAND, DEMANDING TOO LITTLE MONEY, AND MAKING NO DIRECT THREAT AGAINST THE CHILD.

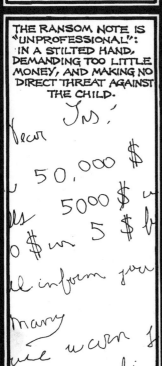

WHY DID THE CRIME OCCUR SO EARLY IN THE EVENING, WHILE THE ENTIRE HOUSE WAS STILL AWAKE?

LINDBERGH ALLOWS HIS WIFE AND HOUSEHOLD STAFF TO BE INTERVIEWED, BUT ONLY TO ESTABLISH THE EVENTS OF LAST EVENING.

AFTER THAT, HE CUTS OFF ACCESS.

A PETTY CRIMINAL NAMED MORRIS "MICKEY" ROSNER, WHO CLAIMS TO HAVE CLOSE CONTACTS IN THE UNDERWORLD, OFFERS HIS SERVICES AS A GO-BETWEEN.

HE INTRODUCES TO COL. LINDBERGH TWO SYMPATHETIC BOOTLEGGERS: SALVATORE "SALVY" SPITALE AND IRVING BITZ.

THESE MEN ARE CERTAIN THAT, AMONG THEM, THEY CAN SECURE THE RELEASE OF THE CHILD.

FROM HIS CELL IN THE COOK COUNTY JAIL IN CHICAGO, THE NATION'S MOST NOTORIOUS GANGSTER OFFERS HIS HELP.

AL CAPONE SYMPATHIZES WITH THE YOUNG FAMILY AND IS CONFIDENT THAT HE CAN RETURN THEIR SON IF THE GOVERNMENT WOULD GRANT HIM HIS FREEDOM. THE OFFER IS RESPECTFULLY DECLINED.

SPITALE AND BITZ ESTABLISH A HEADQUARTERS IN A NEW YORK SPEAK-EASY.

THEY ARE GIVEN TRACINGS OF THE RANSOM NOTE TO AID THEM IN THEIR INQUIRIES.

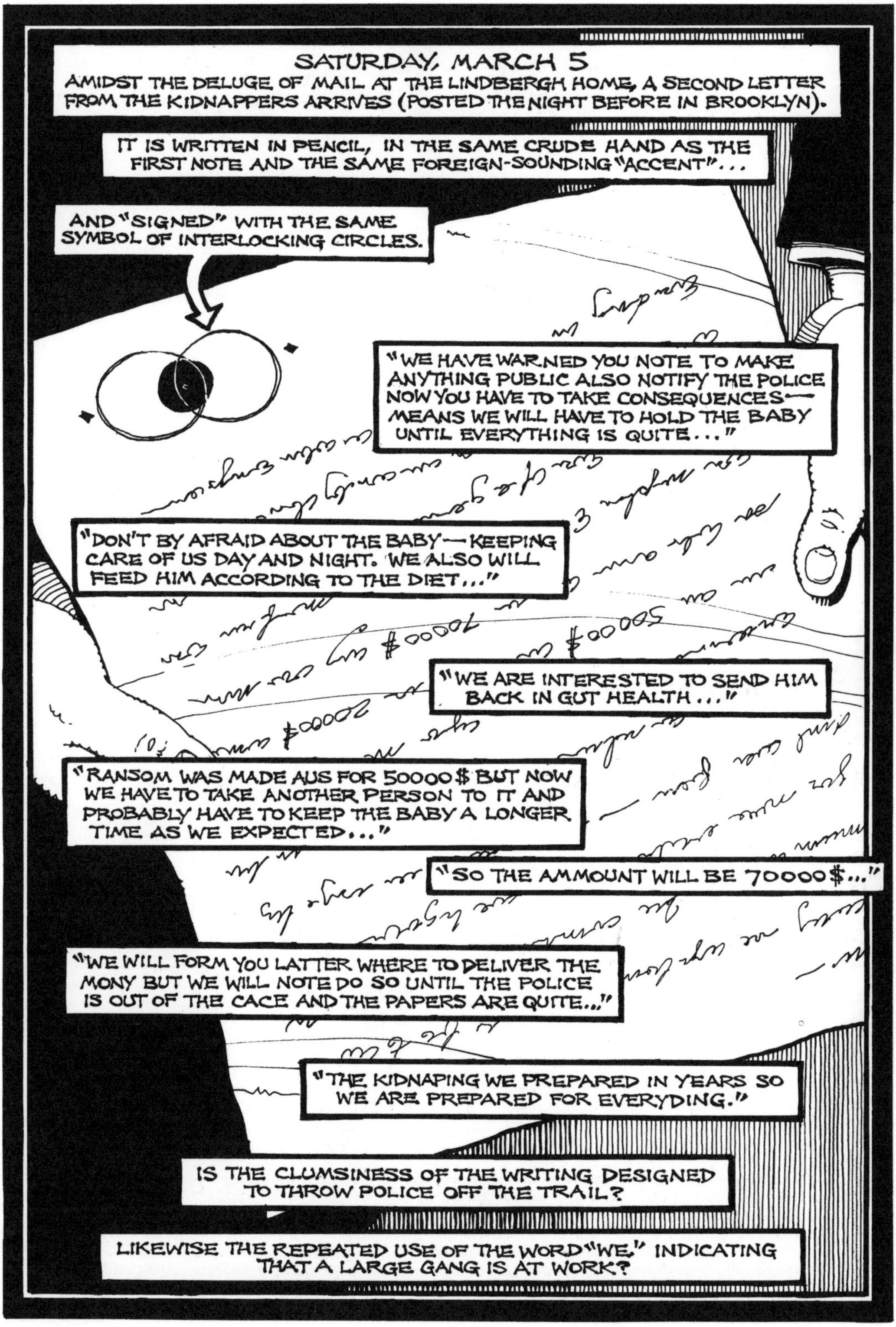
SATURDAY, MARCH 5
AMIDST THE DELUGE OF MAIL AT THE LINDBERGH HOME, A SECOND LETTER FROM THE KIDNAPPERS ARRIVES (POSTED THE NIGHT BEFORE IN BROOKLYN).
IT IS WRITTEN IN PENCIL, IN THE SAME CRUDE HAND AS THE FIRST NOTE AND THE SAME FOREIGN-SOUNDING "ACCENT"...
AND "SIGNED" WITH THE SAME SYMBOL OF INTERLOCKING CIRCLES.
"WE HAVE WARNED YOU NOTE TO MAKE ANYTHING PUBLIC ALSO NOTIFY THE POLICE NOW YOU HAVE TO TAKE CONSEQUENCES— MEANS WE WILL HAVE TO HOLD THE BABY UNTIL EVERYTHING IS QUITE..."
"DON'T BY AFRAID ABOUT THE BABY— KEEPING CARE OF US DAY AND NIGHT. WE ALSO WILL FEED HIM ACCORDING TO THE DIET..."
"WE ARE INTERESTED TO SEND HIM BACK IN GUT HEALTH..."
"RANSOM WAS MADE AUS FOR 50000 $ BUT NOW WE HAVE TO TAKE ANOTHER PERSON TO IT AND PROBABLY HAVE TO KEEP THE BABY A LONGER TIME AS WE EXPECTED..."
"SO THE AMMOUNT WILL BE 70000 $..."
"WE WILL FORM YOU LATTER WHERE TO DELIVER THE MONY BUT WE WILL NOTE DO SO UNTIL THE POLICE IS OUT OF THE CACE AND THE PAPERS ARE QUITE..."
"THE KIDNAPING WE PREPARED IN YEARS SO WE ARE PREPARED FOR EVERYDING."
IS THE CLUMSINESS OF THE WRITING DESIGNED TO THROW POLICE OFF THE TRAIL?
LIKEWISE THE REPEATED USE OF THE WORD "WE," INDICATING THAT A LARGE GANG IS AT WORK?

PART THREE
THE RANSOM

TUESDAY, MARCH 8, 1932
AT THIS POINT, A STRANGE AND COLORFUL
CHARACTER ENTERS THE CASE.

THE BRONX HOME NEWS

DR. JOHN F. CONDON, AGE 72, IS A RETIRED TEACHER, A
PHYSICAL CULTURE DEVOTEE, AND A PROUD AMERICAN.
LIKE MOST CITIZENS, HE IS SHOCKED AND OUTRAGED OVER
THE ABDUCTION OF THE LINDBERGH CHILD.

HE LIVES WITH HIS WIFE MYRA IN THEIR HOME AT 2974 DECATUR AVE.
IN THE NEW YORK BOROUGH OF THE BRONX.

HE IS PARTICULARLY HORRIFIED TO LEARN THAT COL. LINDBERGH IS RELYING UPON PROFESSIONAL CRIMINALS TO FIND HIS CHILD.

HE HAS SUBMITTED A LETTER TO THE LOCAL DAILY NEWSPAPER, THE BRONX HOME NEWS, WHICH IS PUBLISHED IN TODAY'S EDITION.

IN IT, HE ADDRESSES THE KIDNAPPERS, OFFERING HIMSELF AS GO-BETWEEN.

TO SWEETEN THE OFFER, HE PLEDGES $1000 OF HIS OWN MONEY ADDED TO THE RANSOM.

WEDNESDAY, MARCH 9
AN ANSWER ARRIVES AT THE CONDONS' DOOR.

MR. DOCTOR JOHN F. CONDON
2974 DECATUR AVENUE
NEW YORK

CRUDELY LETTERED IN PENCIL, THE NOTE ACCEPTS CONDON AS GO-BETWEEN, WARNS HIM NOT TO NOTIFY THE PRESS OR THE POLICE AND INSTRUCTS HIM TO PLACE AN ANONYMOUS NOTICE IN THE NEW YORK AMERICAN WHEN THE MONEY IS READY.

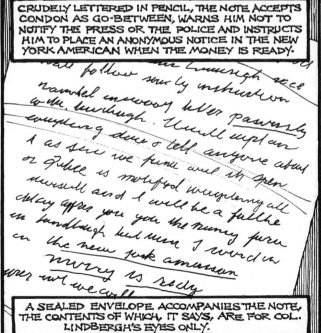

A SEALED ENVELOPE ACCOMPANIES THE NOTE, THE CONTENTS OF WHICH, IT SAYS, ARE FOR COL. LINDBERGH'S EYES ONLY.

CONDON TELEPHONES THE LINDBERGH HOUSE, SPEAKING TO BOTH COL. LINDBERGH AND HENRY BRECKINRIDGE.

THEY ASK HIM TO OPEN AND READ THE SEALED SECOND MESSAGE: IT AUTHORIZES DR. CONDON TO ACT AS GO-BETWEEN...

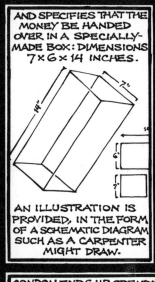

AND SPECIFIES THAT THE MONEY BE HANDED OVER IN A SPECIALLY-MADE BOX: DIMENSIONS 7 x 6 x 14 INCHES.

AN ILLUSTRATION IS PROVIDED, IN THE FORM OF A SCHEMATIC DIAGRAM SUCH AS A CARPENTER MIGHT DRAW.

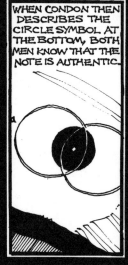

WHEN CONDON THEN DESCRIBES THE CIRCLE SYMBOL AT THE BOTTOM, BOTH MEN KNOW THAT THE NOTE IS AUTHENTIC.

THE OLDER GENTLEMAN IS THEN INVITED OUT TO THE LINDBERGH ESTATE. HE IS DRIVEN THERE BY HIS FRIENDS MILTON GAGLIO AND MAX ROSENHAIN.

ON THE WAY, THEY BECOME LOST SEVERAL TIMES, FINALLY ARRIVING IN THE EARLY HOURS OF THURSDAY, MARCH 10

CONDON ENDS UP SPENDING THE NIGHT ON THE FLOOR OF THE NURSERY...

WHILE HIS FRIENDS ARE SENT BACK TO THE BRONX.

IN THE MORNING, THE LINDBERGHS SIGN A STATEMENT AUTHORIZING HIM AS GO-BETWEEN.

DR. CONDON DESIRES NOTHING MORE THAN TO PERSONALLY DELIVER THE CHILD AGAIN INTO THE EMBRACE OF ITS MOTHER.

AS COL. LINDBERGH FOLLOWS THE RANSOM NOTES, POLICE FOLLOW DIFFERENT AVENUES OF INVESTIGATION.

OF PARTICULAR INTEREST IS THE BOYFRIEND OF BETTY GOW, FINN HENDRIK JOHNSEN, KNOWN AS HENRY "RED" JOHNSEN, A NORWEGIAN SEAMAN ...

WHO WAS TOLD BY HER ON THE NIGHT OF THE KIDNAPPING THAT THE LINDBERGHS WOULD BE REMAINING AT HOPEWELL.

IT TURNS OUT THAT HE HAS WORKED ON SEVERAL LUXURY YACHTS AND IS IN THE UNITED STATES ILLEGALLY ...

AND HE DRIVES A GREEN CAR.

IN THIS CAR IS FOUND AN EMPTY MILK BOTTLE. HE EXPLAINS THAT HE OFTEN DRINKS MILK WHILE DRIVING.

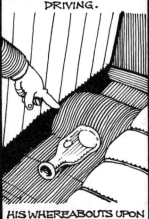

HIS WHEREABOUTS UPON THE NIGHT IN QUESTION— AT HIS BROTHER'S HOUSE IN WEST HARTFORD, CONNECTICUT—SEEM TO BE FIRMLY ESTABLISHED.

THURSDAY, MARCH 10
NEWARK POLICE INTERVIEW THE 29-PERSON STAFF OF NEXT DAY HILL.

ALL OF THEM ARE FOUND TO BE CO-OPERATIVE, EXCEPT FOR MISS VIOLET SHARPE, AN ENGLISH WOMAN, AGE 28, EMPLOYED AS A HOUSEMAID.

SHE IS SAID TO BE ROMANTICALLY INVOLVED WITH THE HEAD BUTLER, SEPTIMUS BANKS.

FOR HER INTERVIEW, SHE APPEARS NERVOUS AND INDIGNANT: WHY SHOULD THE POLICE BE PRYING INTO HER PRIVATE LIFE?

AS TO HER ACTIVITIES ON THE EVENING OF MARCH 1, SHE IS AT FIRST EVASIVE.

SHE THEN RELATES AN IMPLAUSIBLE STORY ABOUT GOING OUT TO A PICTURE SHOW WITH A GROUP OF PEOPLE SHE HAD ONLY MET THAT DAY.

NO, SHE COULD NOT RECALL WHAT PICTURE ... OR THE NAMES OF THE PEOPLE SHE WAS WITH.

FRIDAY, MARCH 11
A CLASSIFIED AD APPEARS IN THE NEW YORK AMERICAN.

I ACCEPT.

MONEY IS READY.

JAFSIE.

THE CODE NAME "JAFSIE" IS MADE UP OF JOHN F. CONDON'S INITIALS.

A REPLY ARRIVES THIS VERY DAY IN THE FORM OF A TELEPHONE CALL. A GUTTURAL VOICE INSTRUCTS DR. CONDON TO REMAIN AT HOME EVERY NIGHT, 6PM TO MIDNIGHT, AND SOON HE WILL RECEIVE ANOTHER NOTE. FOLLOW THE NOTE'S INSTRUCTIONS PRECISELY.

DURING THIS CONVERSATION, CONDON HEARS ANOTHER VOICE IN THE BACKGROUND. TO HIM, IT SOUNDS ITALIAN: "STATTI CITTO!" ("SHUT UP!")

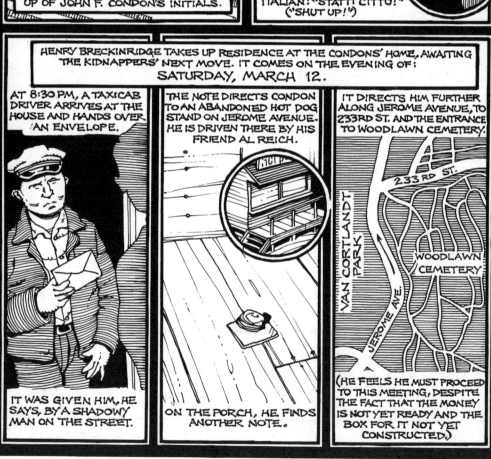

HENRY BRECKINRIDGE TAKES UP RESIDENCE AT THE CONDONS' HOME, AWAITING THE KIDNAPPERS' NEXT MOVE. IT COMES ON THE EVENING OF:
SATURDAY, MARCH 12.

AT 8:30 PM, A TAXICAB DRIVER ARRIVES AT THE HOUSE AND HANDS OVER AN ENVELOPE.

IT WAS GIVEN HIM, HE SAYS, BY A SHADOWY MAN ON THE STREET.

THE NOTE DIRECTS CONDON TO AN ABANDONED HOT DOG STAND ON JEROME AVENUE. HE IS DRIVEN THERE BY HIS FRIEND AL REICH.

ON THE PORCH, HE FINDS ANOTHER NOTE.

IT DIRECTS HIM FURTHER ALONG JEROME AVENUE, TO 233RD ST. AND THE ENTRANCE TO WOODLAWN CEMETERY.

233RD ST.

VAN CORTLANDT PARK

WOODLAWN CEMETERY

JEROME AVE.

(HE FEELS HE MUST PROCEED TO THIS MEETING, DESPITE THE FACT THAT THE MONEY IS NOT YET READY AND THE BOX FOR IT NOT YET CONSTRUCTED.)

DR. CONDON GETS OUT AND WALKS ALONG THE SIDEWALK BESIDE THE CEMETERY. AHEAD, A HAND EMERGES FROM THE BARS, WAVING A HANDKERCHIEF.

(THE ENSUING ENCOUNTER CAN ONLY BE ATTESTED TO BY THE RECOLLECTIONS OF JOHN F. CONDON.)

THE MAN SPEAKS IN A THICK GUTTURAL ACCENT, THE SAME VOICE AS ON THE TELEPHONE EARLIER.

YOU GOTTED THE MONEY WITH YOU?

NO, I CANNOT BRING THE MONEY UNTIL I SEE THE BABY.

THE MAN THEN VAULTS OVER THE FENCE . . .

AND LANDS BESIDE CONDON.

DID YOU BRING THE COPS?

I GAVE YOU MY WORD I WOULDN'T DO THAT.

DR. CONDON FOLLOWS THE STRANGER ACROSS THE STREET, INTO VAN CORTLANDT PARK.

IT'S TOO DANGEROUS!

COME BACK HERE! DON'T BE COWARDLY!

AT LAST, THEY SIT ON A PARK BENCH. THE MAN KEEPS HIS COLLAR UP AND HIS HAT PULLED DOWN, EFFECTIVELY CONCEALING HIS FACE.

IT'S TOO DANGEROUS. MIGHT BE TWENTY YEARS OR BURN. WOULD I BURN IF THE BABY WAS DEAD?

WHAT DO YOU MEAN? WHY WOULD WE BE CARRYING ON NEGOTIATIONS IF THE BABY IS DEAD?

THE BABY IS NOT DEAD THE BABY IS BETTER THAN IT WAS. WE GIVE MORE FOR HIM TO EAT THAN WAS IN THE PAPER. TELL THE COLONEL NOT TO WORRY.

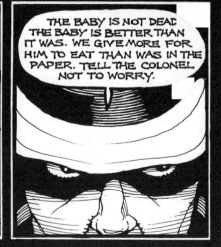

CONDON BRINGS OUT THE SAFETY PINS FROM THE BABY'S BLANKET IN THE NURSERY.

HAVE YOU SEEN THESE?

YES, THOSE PINS FASTENED THE BLANKET TO THE MATTRESS IN THE BABY'S CRIB.

YOU KNOW MY NAME. PLEASE TELL ME YOURS.

JOHN.

WHERE ARE YOU FROM JOHN?

UP FARDER THAN BOSTON.

BIST DU DEUTSCH?

NO, I AM SCANDINAVIAN.

 "JOHN" EXPLAINS THAT HE IS MERELY A GO-BETWEEN. THE PLOT IS HEADED BY A MAN HE CALLS "NUMBER ONE," WHO WAS ONCE A HIGH OFFICIAL IN THE GOVERNMENT. "NUMBER TWO" IS A MAN WHO KNOWS DR. CONDON WELL AND BELIEVES HIM TO BE A FINE PERSON.
THE BABY, HE SAYS, IS SAFE ABOARD A BOAT, BEING TAKEN CARE OF BY TWO WOMEN.

LOOK, JOHN, LEAVE THEM! COME WITH ME TO MY HOUSE. I WILL GIVE YOU ONE THOUSAND DOLLARS. THEN I WILL TAKE YOU OUT TO JERSEY TO SEE COL. LINDBERGH. THAT WAY YOU CAN BE ON THE SIDE OF THE LAW.

NO! THEY WOULD SMACK ME OUT! THEY WOULD DRILL ME!

DON'T YOU SEE? SOONER OR LATER YOU WILL BE CAUGHT.

OH, NO! WE HAVE PLANNED THIS CASE FOR A YEAR ALREADY.

I GO NOW... I HAVE STAYED TOO LONG ALREADY. NUMBER ONE WILL BE MAD. I SHOULD HAVE GOTTED THE MONEY.

I WILL SEND BY MONDAY MORNING A TOKEN.

AS THEY PART, THE MEN AGREE TO COMMUNICATE AGAIN THROUGH NEWSPAPER ADS AND COMPLETE THE TRANSACTION ON A "CASH AND DELIVERY" BASIS.

SUNDAY, MARCH 13

POLICE BRING TO THE LINDBERGH HOME DR. ERASMUS M. HUDSON, PHYSICIAN AND FINGERPRINT EXPERT, IN THE HOPE THAT HE CAN FIND PRINTS WHERE THE POLICE TECHNICIAN DID NOT.

DR. HUDSON SPRAYS THE BABY'S TOYS WITH A FINE MIST OF SILVER NITRATE, AND THEN EXPOSES THEM TO THE SUN.

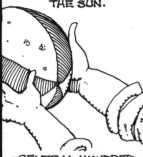

SEVERAL HUNDRED PARTIAL PRINTS EMERGE, OF WHICH THIRTEEN ARE IDENTIFIABLE AS THOSE OF THE CHILD.

THE KIDNAP LADDER UNDERGOES THE SAME PROCESS. OVER 500 SMUDGES ARE FOUND, OF WHICH 200 ARE USABLE PRINTS...

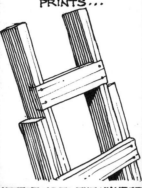

ATTESTING TO THE NUMBER OF OFFICIALS WHO HAVE SULLIED THIS IMPORTANT ITEM OF EVIDENCE.

PAINSTAKING SCRUTINY OF THE NURSERY REVEALS NO PRINTS FROM THE LINDBERGHS OR THEIR HOUSEHOLD STAFF.

THE SURFACES OF THE ROOM, IN FACT, APPEAR TO HAVE BEEN WIPED CLEAN.

TUESDAY, MARCH 15

ON THIS DAY, A PARCEL ARRIVES AT THE CONDON HOME. HENRY BRECKINRIDGE HURRIES THERE TO OPEN IT.

INSIDE IS A BABY'S SLEEPING SUIT — UNDOUBTEDLY THE "TOKEN" PROMISED BY THE MAN IN THE CEMETERY.

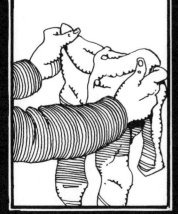

COL. LINDBERGH — IN DISGUISE — ARRIVES EARLY THE NEXT MORNING.

THE GARMENT HAS APPARENTLY BEEN LAUNDERED, BUT HE THINKS THAT, IN ALL PROBABILITY, IT IS HIS SON'S.

A NOTE IS ENCLOSED WITH THE SUIT DEMANDING THAT AN AD BE PLACED IN THE NEW YORK AMERICAN WHEN THE MONEY IS READY. THEN...

"AFTER 8 HOURS WE HAVE THE MONY RECEIVED, WE WILL NOTIFY YOU WHERE TO FIND THE BABY. IF THERE IS ANY TRAPP, YOU WILL BE RESPONSIBLE FOR WHAT FOLLOWS."

WEDNESDAY, MARCH 16
A SECOND CLASSIFIED AD RUNS IN THE NEW YORK AMERICAN.

I ACCEPT
MONEY IS READY.
JOHN, YOUR PACKAGE IS DELIVERED AND IS OK. DIRECT ME.
JAFSIE

DURING THIS TIME, COL. LINDBERGH HAS BEEN SELLING STOCKS AND BONDS, CLOSING OUT ACCOUNTS TO ACCUMULATE THE NECESSARY CASH.

A WOODEN BOX, BUILT TO THE KIDNAPPERS' SPECIFICATIONS, HAS BEEN COMPLETED BY A LOCAL CABINETMAKER.

MONDAY, MARCH 21
A LETTER IS AT LAST DELIVERED TO DR. CONDON...

"YOU AND MR. LINDBERGH KNOW OUR PROGRAM. IF YOU DON'T ACCEPT DEN WE WILL WAIT UNTIL YOU AGREE WITH OUR DEAL."

"WE WILL TELL YOU AGAIN: THIS KIDNAPPING CACE WAS PREPARED FOR A YEAR ALREADY SO THE POLICE WON'T HAVE ANY LUCK TO FIND US OR THE CHILD."

DID THE KIDNAPPERS MISS LAST WEEK'S AD? THEY SEEM TO THINK THAT LINDBERGH DOES NOT ACCEPT THEIR TERMS.

CONDON AND BRECKINRIDGE COMPOSE ANOTHER AD...
IT RUNS IN THE NEW YORK AMERICAN AND THE BRONX HOME NEWS FOR THREE CONSECUTIVE DAYS.

THANKS.
THAT LITTLE PACKAGE YOU SENT ME WAS IMMEDIATELY DELIVERED AND ACCEPTED AS THE REAL ARTICLE. SEE MY POSITION. OVER FIFTY YEARS IN BUSINESS AND CAN I PAY WITHOUT SEEING THE GOODS? COMMON SENSE MAKES ME TRUST YOU. CASE UNDERSTAND MY
JAFSIE.

THE CASH IS COLLECTED INTO THE DENOMINATIONS DEMANDED BY THE KIDNAPPERS.

ALSO IN ACCORDANCE WITH THEIR WISHES, COL. LINDBERGH REFUSES TO HAVE THE BILLS MARKED IN ANY WAY. HE IS CONVINCED, HOWEVER, BY AGENTS OF THE BUREAU OF INVESTIGATION TO HAVE THE SERIAL NUMBERS RECORDED.

ALSO AT THIS TIME, A NEW AVENUE TO THE KIDNAPPERS EMERGES, IN THE PERSON OF JOHN H. CURTIS, AGE 43, A WEALTHY AND RESPECTED BOAT-BUILDER OF NORFOLK, VIRGINIA.

TUESDAY, MARCH 22

HE COMES TO THE LINDBERGH ESTATE IN THE COMPANY OF TWO LIKEWISE RESPECTABLE CITIZENS: ADMIRAL GUY BURRAGE AND THE REVEREND HAROLD DOBSON-PEACOCK, BOTH OF THEM ACQUAINTANCES OF THE LINDBERGH AND MORROW FAMILIES.

CURTIS RELATES TO COL. LINDBERGH A STRANGE AND COMPELLING STORY...

IT SEEMS THAT, BACK ON MARCH 9, HE WAS ACCOSTED BY A MYSTERIOUS MAN CALLING HIMSELF "SAM."

THE MAN EXPLAINED THAT HE WAS AN ASSOCIATE OF THE SCANDINAVIAN GANG THAT HAD STOLEN THE LINDBERGH BABY...

AND THAT THEY HAD CHOSEN CURTIS TO ACT AS A CONDUIT TO COL. LINDBERGH.

CURTIS WAS SHOCKED AND SPENT A NIGHT OF INDECISION.

THE NEXT MORNING, HE TOLD "SAM" THAT HE WOULD ACCEPT THE TASK.

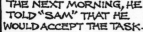

COL. LINDBERGH HAS DOUBTS ABOUT THE STORY. COULD THESE BE THE SAME PEOPLE WHO CONTACTED DR. CONDON?

STILL, HE DOES NOT WANT TO CLOSE OFF ANY POSSIBILITY. HE ASKS CURTIS TO DEMAND FROM "SAM" PROOF THAT THE CHILD IS WELL—SUCH AS A RECENT PHOTOGRAPH.

AS THE MONTH OF MARCH CLOSES, YET A THIRD CONNECTION TO THE KIDNAPPERS IS IN PLAY...

INITIATED BY GASTON B. MEANS, AGE 53, A FORMER PRIVATE DETECTIVE AND AGENT FOR THE BUREAU OF INVESTIGATION.

THOUGH OF UNSAVORY REPUTATION, HE HAS MANAGED TO GAIN THE TRUST OF THE WEALTHY WASHINGTON HOSTESS EVALYN WALSH McLEAN, A FRIEND OF THE LINDBERGHS.

MEANS HAS TOLD HER OF HOW, BEFORE THE CRIME, HE WAS APPROACHED BY THE KIDNAP GANG AND ASKED TO JOIN THEM.

HE REFUSED, BUT WAS NOW APPOINTED TO HANDLE THE NEGOTIATIONS.

WITH COL. LINDBERGH'S APPROVAL, MRS. McLEAN HAS HANDED OVER $50,000 OF HER OWN MONEY TO PAY THE RANSOM.

THIS IS SHORTLY RAISED TO $100,000.

MEANS HAS COLLECTED THE FULL SUM FROM HER, IN CASH — PLUS FURTHER AMOUNTS FOR HIS EXPENSES.

MRS. McLEAN NOW WAITS PATIENTLY WHILE HE GIVES HER EXCUSE AFTER EXCUSE AS TO WHY THE EXCHANGE CANNOT BE MADE.

FRIDAY, APRIL 1
WHILE WALKING ABOUT THE ESTATE, BETTY GOW AND ELSIE WHATELEY MAKE A SURPRISING DISCOVERY:

ONE OF THE BABY'S THUMB-GUARDS, LYING ALONG THE EDGE OF THE GRAVEL DRIVEWAY LEADING TO THE HOUSE.

DOES THIS MEAN THAT THE KIDNAPPERS USED THE MAIN DRIVEWAY AS THEIR ESCAPE ROUTE, RATHER THAN THE WOODS TO THE EAST?

FURTHER, COULD THE THUMB-GUARD HAVE LAIN THERE UNNOTICED FOR SO LONG BESIDE THE HEAVILY-TRAVELLED DRIVEWAY?

SATURDAY, APRIL 2
COL. LINDBERGH AND HENRY BRECKINRIDGE WAIT AT THE CONDONS' HOUSE FOR A RESPONSE TO THEIR ADVERTISEMENT.

AT ABOUT 7:45 PM, A TAXI DRIVER, AS BEFORE, LEAVES AN ENVELOPE ON THE FRONT PORCH.

THIS TIME, COL. LINDBERGH ACCOMPANIES THE DOCTOR.

OF THE $70,000 GATHERED, JUST $50,000 WILL FIT INTO THE SPECIALLY-BUILT CONTAINER.

THE NOTE DIRECTS THEM TO A GREENHOUSE AND NURSERY ON TREMONT AVENUE.

AT THE NURSERY, ANOTHER NOTE IS WAITING ON A TABLE OUTSIDE. IT SENDS THEM FURTHER EAST, TO ANOTHER CEMETERY: ST. RAYMOND'S.

THEY STOP AT THE CEMETERY'S ENTRANCE. CONDON GETS OUT, LEAVING LINDBERGH IN THE CAR.

BUT HE HESITATES TO ENTER THE DARK AND THREATENING INTERIOR.

A VOICE CALLS FROM THE DARKNESS, HEARD PLAINLY BY BOTH MEN.

HEY, DOCTOR— OVER HERE!

CONDON, DECIDING NOT TO CARRY THE BOX OF MONEY FOLLOWS THE VOICE INTO THE CEMETERY...

WHILE THE LONE EAGLE CAN DO NOTHING BUT WAIT.

SUDDENLY, A MAN POPS UP FROM BEHIND A TOMBSTONE.

HERE, DOCTOR!

THE MAN LEADS CONDON DEEPER INTO THE CEMETERY. AT LAST THEY SPEAK WITH A HEDGE BETWEEN THEM. THE DOCTOR RECOGNIZES HIM AS THE SAME "JOHN" HE SPOKE WITH BEFORE.

YOU GOT IT, THE MONEY?

NO, IT'S UP IN THE CAR.

WHO IS UP THERE?

COL. LINDBERGH.

CONDON REFUSES TO GIVE UP THE MONEY WITHOUT A "RECEIPT" TELLING WHERE THE CHILD IS.

"JOHN" GOES OFF TO GET ONE WHILE CONDON RETURNS TO THE CAR FOR THE BOX OF CASH.

FIFTEEN MINUTES LATER, THEY FIND EACH OTHER AGAIN. BY CONDON'S WATCH: 9:29 PM.

NOW GIVE ME THE NOTE.

DON'T OPEN IT YET, NOT FOR SIX HOURS.

THE TWO MEN, ONCE AGAIN, SHAKE HANDS AND PART.

IF YOU GIVE ME A CHANCE TO GET THAT BABY, EVERYTHING WILL BE ALL RIGHT BUT IF YOU DON'T, I WILL FOLLOW YOU TO AUSTRALIA. DON'T TRY TO DOUBLE-CROSS ME.

BACK AT THE CAR, CONDON GIVES THE ENVELOPE TO LINDBERGH.

I PROMISED NOT TO OPEN IT FOR SIX HOURS, BUT THAT DOESN'T MEAN THAT YOU CAN'T.

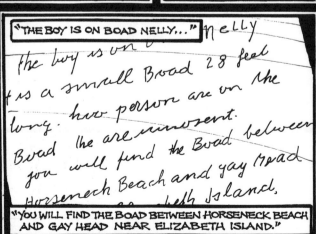

"THE BOY IS ON BOAD NELLY..."

"YOU WILL FIND THE BOAD BETWEEN HORSENECK BEACH AND GAY HEAD NEAR ELIZABETH ISLAND."

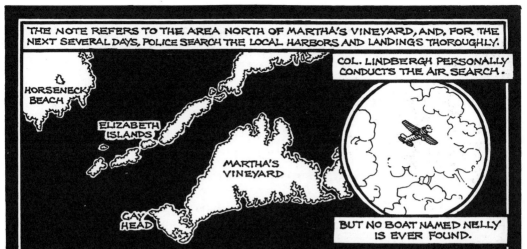

THE NOTE REFERS TO THE AREA NORTH OF MARTHA'S VINEYARD, AND, FOR THE NEXT SEVERAL DAYS, POLICE SEARCH THE LOCAL HARBORS AND LANDINGS THOROUGHLY.

HORSENECK BEACH

ELIZABETH ISLANDS

MARTHA'S VINEYARD

GAY HEAD

COL. LINDBERGH PERSONALLY CONDUCTS THE AIR SEARCH.

BUT NO BOAT NAMED NELLY IS EVER FOUND.

WEDNESDAY, APRIL 6
THE UNITED STATES TREASURY DEPARTMENT BEGINS TO CIRCULATE A LIST OF THE RECORDED RANSOM BILLS TO BANKS ACROSS THE NATION.

TWO DAYS LATER, THE FIRST OF THE NOTES TURNS UP AT A BANK IN THE BRONX.

NO FURTHER MESSAGES ARE RECEIVED BY JOHN F. CONDON, BUT LINDBERGH REFUSES TO GIVE UP HOPE.

HE RETURNS HIS ATTENTION TO THE AVENUE OFFERED BY JOHN H. CURTIS.

CURTIS CLAIMS THAT, THROUGH HIS CONTACT "SAM," HE HAS MET WITH THE CAPTAIN OF THE SCHOONER ON WHICH THE CHILD IS BEING KEPT.

AMONG THE GROUP IS A MAN CALLED "JOHN," WHO SPEAKS WITH A HEAVY ACCENT.

FOR THE NEXT SEVERAL WEEKS, RENDEZVOUS POINTS ARE ARRANGED, ONLY FOR THEM TO FALL THROUGH AT THE LAST MOMENT.

ALSO BY THIS TIME, THE SCHEME INITIATED BY GASTON MEANS HAS BEGUN TO UNRAVEL. HAVING LED MRS. McLEAN AROUND THE COUNTRY—TO SOUTH CAROLINA AND TEXAS—HE KEEPS REASSURING HER THAT THEY ARE ON THE VERY BRINK OF FINDING THE CHILD.

BY THE END OF APRIL, HOWEVER, SHE HAS GROWN WEARY OF THE CHASE AND DEMANDS THAT HER MONEY BE RETURNED.

IN THE MEANTIME, THE PRESS HAS GOTTEN WIND OF THE FACT THAT THE RANSOM HAS BEEN PAID BUT THE CHILD NOT RETURNED.

MONDAY, APRIL 11
THE NEW YORK TIMES REVEALS THAT THE MYSTERIOUS "JAFSIE" IS DR. JOHN F. CONDON OF THE BRONX.

CROWDS SURROUND HIS HOME ON DECATUR AVENUE. AT FIRST HE BASKS IN THE CELEBRITY...

BUT SOON HE MUST OBTAIN AN UNLISTED TELEPHONE NUMBER.

AT POLICE HEADQUARTERS, HE PERUSES COUNTLESS "MUG" SHOTS.

A POLICE ARTIST DRAWS A SKETCH FROM HIS DESCRIPTION OF "JOHN."

WEDNESDAY, APRIL 13
AN OFFICER OF THE STATE POLICE CONDUCTS A SECOND INTERVIEW WITH VIOLET SHARPE, HOUSEMAID AT NEXT DAY HILL.

SHE IS NO LESS ANGRY AND EVASIVE THAN DURING HER FIRST, MORE THAN A MONTH AGO.

HER STORY HAS CHANGED SOMEWHAT: SHE DID NOT ATTEND A PICTURE SHOW ON MARCH 1, SHE SAYS, BUT WENT TO A ROADHOUSE CALLED THE PEANUT GRILL.

HER COMPANION WAS A MAN NAMED "ERNIE," WHOM SHE HAD MET THAT DAY. NO, SHE CANNOT REMEMBER HIS LAST NAME.

TO THE POLICE, HER STORY STILL RINGS HOLLOW. ISN'T SHE PRACTICALLY ENGAGED TO THE BUTLER SEPTIMUS BANKS?

A SEARCH OF HER ROOM FINDS A STACK OF BUSINESS CARDS FROM A LOCAL TAXICAB SERVICE.

THURSDAY, MAY 12 ON THIS DAY, EVERYTHING CHANGES.

HOPEWELL

JUST OUTSIDE OF HOPEWELL, THEY STOP BY THE ROAD SO THAT ALLEN CAN RELIEVE HIMSELF IN THE WOODS.

A TRUCK DRIVER, ORVILLE WILSON, AND HIS ASSISTANT, WILLIAM ALLEN, DRIVE NORTHWARD ON THE PRINCETON-HOPEWELL ROAD.

HE WALKS TO THE TOP OF A RISE AND THERE COMES UPON, TO HIS HORROR, WHAT LOOK LIKE THE BADLY DECOMPOSED REMAINS OF A SMALL CHILD.

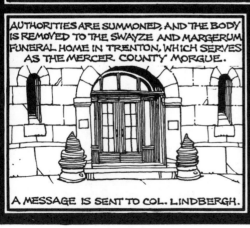

AUTHORITIES ARE SUMMONED, AND THE BODY IS REMOVED TO THE SWAYZE AND MARGERUM FUNERAL HOME IN TRENTON, WHICH SERVES AS THE MERCER COUNTY MORGUE.

A MESSAGE IS SENT TO COL. LINDBERGH.

AT THIS MOMENT, THE AVIATOR IS ABOARD JOHN CURTIS' YACHT, THE "CACHALOT" OFF CAPE MAY, NEW JERSEY — IN HOPES OF A MEETING WITH THE KIDNAPPERS.

THEY HAVE REPEATEDLY ASSURED HIM, THROUGH CURTIS, THAT HIS SON IS IN FINE HEALTH.

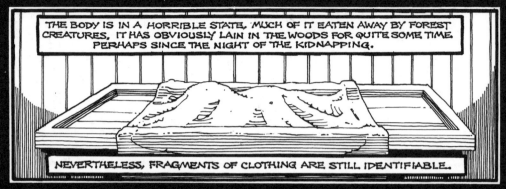

THE BODY IS IN A HORRIBLE STATE, MUCH OF IT EATEN AWAY BY FOREST CREATURES, IT HAS OBVIOUSLY LAIN IN THE WOODS FOR QUITE SOME TIME. PERHAPS SINCE THE NIGHT OF THE KIDNAPPING.

NEVERTHELESS, FRAGMENTS OF CLOTHING ARE STILL IDENTIFIABLE.

BETTY GOW RECOGNIZES THE FABRIC AND THREAD SHE USED TO SEW THE BABY A NIGHTSHIRT ON THE EVENING OF THE CRIME.

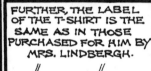

FURTHER, THE LABEL OF THE T-SHIRT IS THE SAME AS IN THOSE PURCHASED FOR HIM BY MRS. LINDBERGH.

COL. LINDBERGH SADLY IDENTIFIES HIS SON THROUGH CERTAIN UNMISTAKABLE PHYSICAL CHARACTERISTICS.

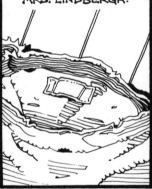

THE AUTOPSY CONCLUDES THAT THE BOY MET HIS DEATH BY A FRACTURE OF THE SKULL CAUSED BY EXTERNAL VIOLENCE.

SPECULATION ARISES THAT THE CHILD WAS DROPPED ACCIDENTALLY AS IT WAS BEING CARRIED DOWN THE LADDER, PERHAPS IN A BAG OF SOME SORT...

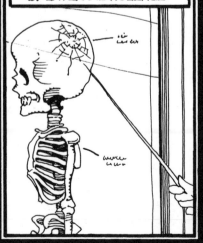

THE THIRTY POUNDS OF EXTRA WEIGHT CAUSING THE FLIMSY LADDER TO BREAK AT ITS LEAST STABLE JUNCTURE.

PART FOUR
THE MANHUNT

THE SHOCKING NEWS SPREADS THROUGHOUT THE WORLD. THE CASE OF KIDNAPPING IS NOW ONE OF MURDER.

COL. LINDBERGH NOW RELINQUISHES HIS LEADING ROLE IN THE INVESTIGATION. HE AND HIS WIFE — NOW PREGNANT WITH THEIR SECOND CHILD — GO INTO DEEP SECLUSION.

THE MANHUNT IS NOW TAKEN UP IN EARNEST BY THE NEW JERSEY STATE POLICE, COMMANDED BY COL. H. NORMAN SCHWARZKOPF, ASSISTED BY LOCAL AGENCIES OF A SEVERAL-STATE AREA.

HE WILL EVENTUALLY BE TRIED FOR FRAUD.

GASTON MEANS WILL ALSO BE PUT ON TRIAL FOR HIS DEVIOUS EXTORTION OF MONEY FROM MRS. EVALYN McLEAN.

THE LADY WILL SEE ONLY A FRACTION OF IT RETURNED TO HER.

THE UNFORTUNATE VIOLET SHARPE COMES TO A BAD END.

THURSDAY, JUNE 9
SHE IDENTIFIES A PHOTOGRAPH OF A TAXI-SERVICE OPERATOR NAMED ERNEST BRINKERT AS THE MAN WITH WHOM SHE WENT TO THE ROADHOUSE.

SHE THEN BECOMES HYSTERICAL AND REFUSES TO ANSWER ANY FURTHER QUESTIONS.

POLICE PLAN TO RETURN THE NEXT DAY, BUT BEFORE THEY CAN...

FRIDAY, JUNE 10
VIOLET SHARPE COMMITS SUICIDE BY SWALLOWING A MIXTURE OF WATER AND CYANIDE CHLORIDE, IN THE FORM OF A POWDERED SILVER POLISH.

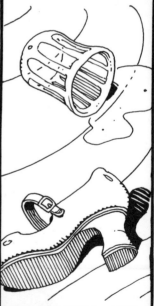

HER ACTIVITIES ON THE NIGHT OF THE KIDNAPPING ARE LATER FOUND TO HAVE BEEN PERFECTLY INNOCENT, LEAVING ANOTHER MYSTERY AMONG THE MANY IN THIS CASE.

DURING THE SUMMER OF 1932, THE LINDBERGHS LEAVE THE HOUSE AT HOPEWELL, NEVER TO RESIDE THERE AGAIN.

WEDNESDAY, JUNE 22 CONGRESS PASSES THE "LINDBERGH LAW," MAKING KIDNAPPING A FEDERAL CRIME — ALTHOUGH TOO LATE TO HELP IN THIS CASE.

TUESDAY, AUGUST 16 IN NEW YORK CITY, ANNE LINDBERGH GIVES BIRTH TO THEIR SECOND CHILD, A SON THEY NAME JON.

THE WRITTEN MESSAGES FROM THE KIDNAPPER — THIRTEEN IN ALL — HAVE BEEN PLACED UNDER THE SCRUTINY OF SEVERAL HANDWRITING EXPERTS...

INCLUDING PROF. ALBERT OSBORNE, CALLED THE DEAN OF AMERICAN FORENSIC GRAPHOLOGISTS.

THEIR CONSENSUS IS THAT THE NOTES WERE ALL WRITTEN BY THE SAME HAND. THE MISSPELLINGS AND GRAMMATICAL ANOMALIES ARE CONSISTENT THROUGHOUT.

THE WRITER IS MOST LIKELY GERMAN.

THE MESSAGES ARE ALSO STUDIED BY A NEW YORK PSYCHIATRIST, DR. DUDLEY SCHOENFELD.

HIS CONCLUSIONS:

THE KIDNAPPER IS A MAN WITH DELUSIONS OF OMNIPOTENCE, WHO NEVERTHELESS OCCUPIES A LOW STATION IN LIFE...

AND BLAMES OTHERS FOR HIS FAILURES AND INADEQUACIES.

THIS MAN FOCUSES ALL OF HIS ANGER AND FRUSTRATION ON COL. LINDBERGH, THE UNIVERSALLY ADORED HERO, AND SCHEMES TO OUTSMART AND HUMILIATE HIM.

SUCH A MAN WOULD WORK ALONE AND TAKE GREAT PERSONAL RISKS.

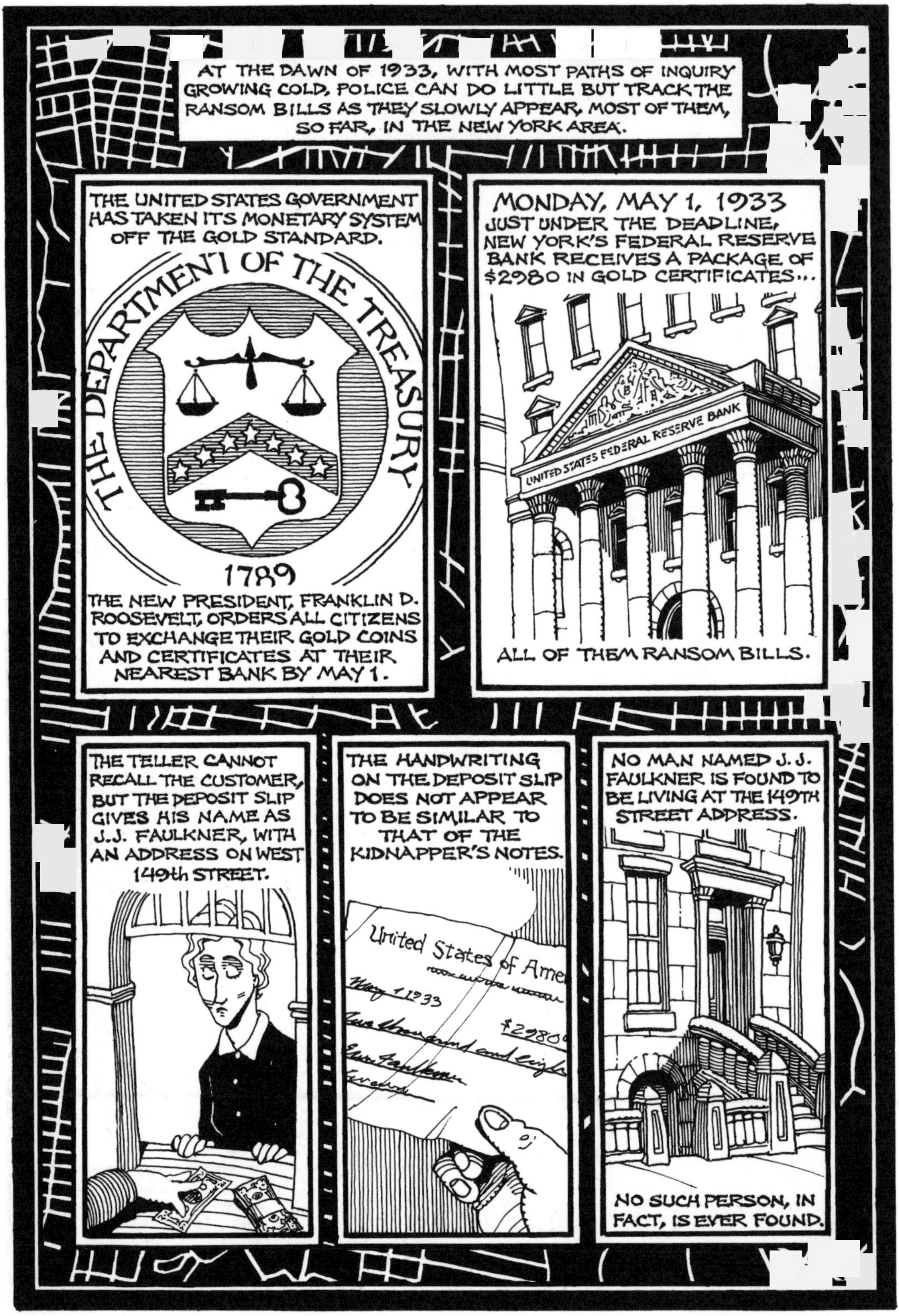
AT THE DAWN OF 1933, WITH MOST PATHS OF INQUIRY GROWING COLD, POLICE CAN DO LITTLE BUT TRACK THE RANSOM BILLS AS THEY SLOWLY APPEAR. MOST OF THEM, SO FAR, IN THE NEW YORK AREA.
THE UNITED STATES GOVERNMENT HAS TAKEN ITS MONETARY SYSTEM OFF THE GOLD STANDARD.
THE DEPARTMENT OF THE TREASURY
1789
THE NEW PRESIDENT, FRANKLIN D. ROOSEVELT, ORDERS ALL CITIZENS TO EXCHANGE THEIR GOLD COINS AND CERTIFICATES AT THEIR NEAREST BANK BY MAY 1.
MONDAY, MAY 1, 1933
JUST UNDER THE DEADLINE, NEW YORK'S FEDERAL RESERVE BANK RECEIVES A PACKAGE OF $2980 IN GOLD CERTIFICATES...
UNITED STATES FEDERAL RESERVE BANK
ALL OF THEM RANSOM BILLS.
THE TELLER CANNOT RECALL THE CUSTOMER, BUT THE DEPOSIT SLIP GIVES HIS NAME AS J.J. FAULKNER, WITH AN ADDRESS ON WEST 149th STREET.
THE HANDWRITING ON THE DEPOSIT SLIP DOES NOT APPEAR TO BE SIMILAR TO THAT OF THE KIDNAPPER'S NOTES.
United States of Ame
May 1 1933
$2980
NO MAN NAMED J. J. FAULKNER IS FOUND TO BE LIVING AT THE 149TH STREET ADDRESS.
NO SUCH PERSON, IN FACT, IS EVER FOUND.

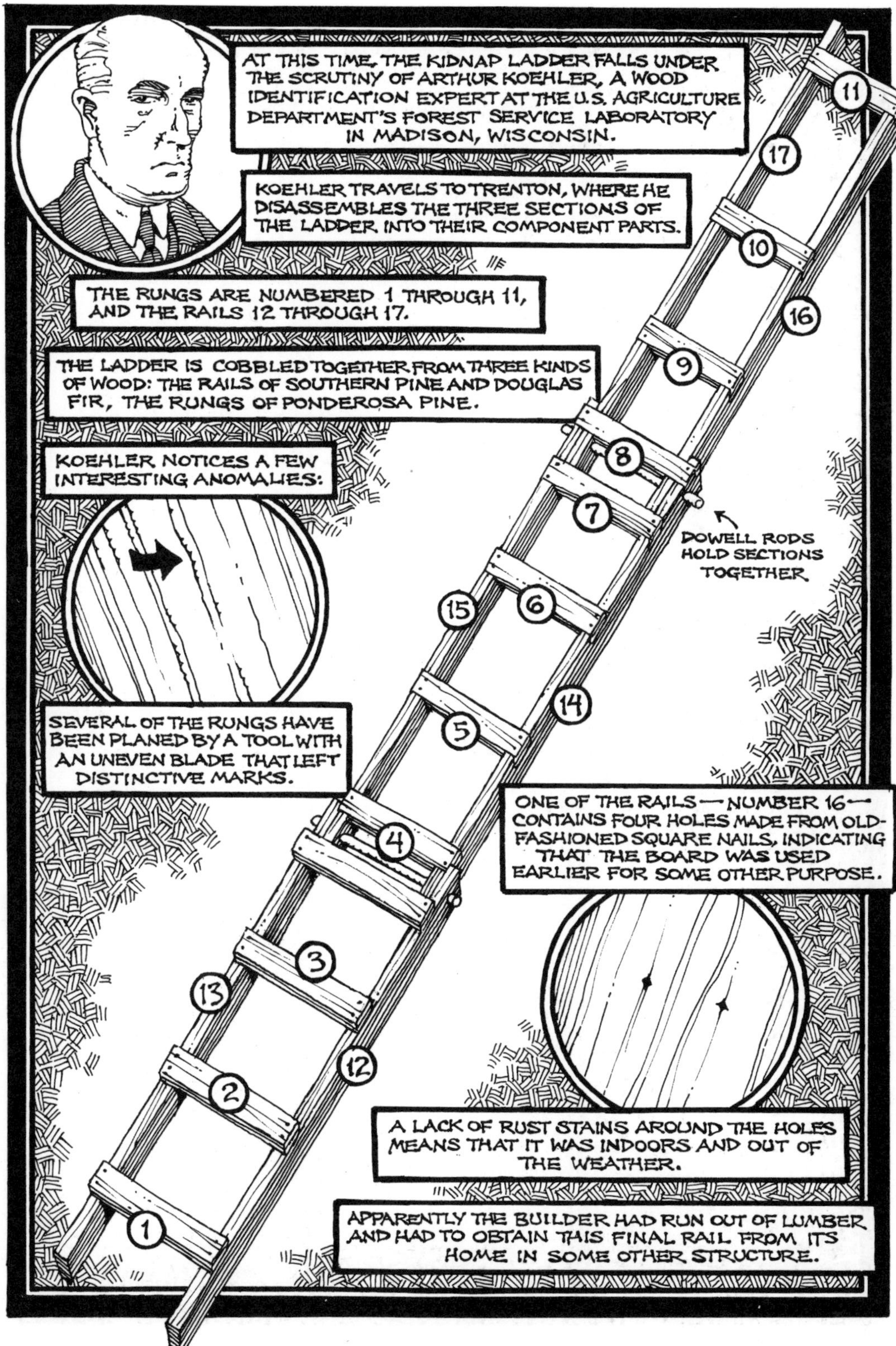
AT THIS TIME, THE KIDNAP LADDER FALLS UNDER THE SCRUTINY OF ARTHUR KOEHLER, A WOOD IDENTIFICATION EXPERT AT THE U.S. AGRICULTURE DEPARTMENT'S FOREST SERVICE LABORATORY IN MADISON, WISCONSIN.
KOEHLER TRAVELS TO TRENTON, WHERE HE DISASSEMBLES THE THREE SECTIONS OF THE LADDER INTO THEIR COMPONENT PARTS.
THE RUNGS ARE NUMBERED 1 THROUGH 11, AND THE RAILS 12 THROUGH 17.
THE LADDER IS COBBLED TOGETHER FROM THREE KINDS OF WOOD: THE RAILS OF SOUTHERN PINE AND DOUGLAS FIR, THE RUNGS OF PONDEROSA PINE.
KOEHLER NOTICES A FEW INTERESTING ANOMALIES:
SEVERAL OF THE RUNGS HAVE BEEN PLANED BY A TOOL WITH AN UNEVEN BLADE THAT LEFT DISTINCTIVE MARKS.
11
17
10
16
9
8
7
DOWELL RODS HOLD SECTIONS TOGETHER
15
6
14
5
4
3
13
12
2
1
ONE OF THE RAILS — NUMBER 16 — CONTAINS FOUR HOLES MADE FROM OLD-FASHIONED SQUARE NAILS, INDICATING THAT THE BOARD WAS USED EARLIER FOR SOME OTHER PURPOSE.
A LACK OF RUST STAINS AROUND THE HOLES MEANS THAT IT WAS INDOORS AND OUT OF THE WEATHER.
APPARENTLY THE BUILDER HAD RUN OUT OF LUMBER AND HAD TO OBTAIN THIS FINAL RAIL FROM ITS HOME IN SOME OTHER STRUCTURE.

IN THE SIDE-RAILS MADE OF SOUTHERN PINE, KOEHLER DISCERNS THE MARKINGS OF A DEFECTIVE BLADE IN THE PLANING PROCESS AT THE SAWMILL WHERE THE LUMBER ORIGINATED.

HE BEGINS A LABORIOUS INVESTIGATION INTO THE SOURCE OF THE PINE BOARDS.

AS A FIRST STEP, HE SENDS A FORM LETTER TO EVERY LUMBER MILL ON THE EASTERN SEABOARD, 1598 IN ALL.

TWENTY-FIVE MILLS RESPOND THAT, YES, THEY USE THE KIND OF PLANERS THAT KOEHLER DESCRIBES.

HE REQUESTS FROM THESE MILLS SMALL SAMPLES OF THE LUMBER RUN THROUGH THE PLANERS TWO YEARS AGO.

WOOD FROM A MILL IN SOUTH CAROLINA SHOWS REMARKABLE SIMILARITIES TO THE BOARDS IN THE LADDER.

KOEHLER TRAVELS TO THE MILL, AND, AFTER MUCH TESTING, CONCLUDES THAT THE LADDER'S RAILS WERE MILLED THERE AFTER SEPTEMBER, 1929.

HE THEN SPENDS SEVERAL MONTHS FOLLOWING EVERY SHIPMENT OF 1"x 4" SOUTHERN PINE BOARDS FROM THE MILL TO RETAILERS IN THE NORTHEAST.

ONE LUMBER YARD AFTER ANOTHER TELLS HIM THAT THEIR STOCK FROM THAT TIME PERIOD HAS SOLD OUT.

AT LAST, THE TRAIL BRINGS HIM TO THE NATIONAL LUMBER AND MILLWORK CO. IN THE WILLIAMSBRIDGE SECTION OF THE BRONX.

SOME BOARDS FROM THAT TIME HAPPEN TO HAVE BEEN SAVED. KOEHLER DECLARES THEM TO BE THE SAME AS THOSE USED IN THE LADDER.

THE LUMBER YARD HAS NO RECORD OF WHO BOUGHT THE WOOD TWO YEARS AGO, SO HERE THE INVESTIGATION STALLS.

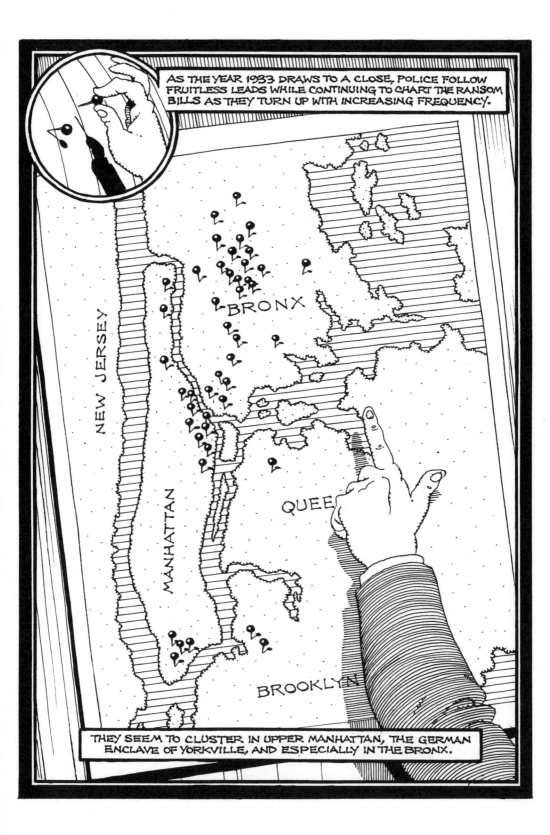

AS THE YEAR 1933 DRAWS TO A CLOSE, POLICE FOLLOW FRUITLESS LEADS WHILE CONTINUING TO CHART THE RANSOM BILLS AS THEY TURN UP WITH INCREASING FREQUENCY.

THEY SEEM TO CLUSTER IN UPPER MANHATTAN, THE GERMAN ENCLAVE OF YORKVILLE, AND ESPECIALLY IN THE BRONX.

SUNDAY, NOVEMBER 26

THE CASHIER AT A GREENWICH VILLAGE PICTURE HOUSE IS CONFRONTED BY AN UNUSUAL CUSTOMER.

IN A HEAVY ACCENT, HE ASKS FOR A SINGLE TICKET AND TOSSES HER A SMALL SQUARE OF PAPER.

IT IS A $5.00 BILL, TIGHTLY FOLDED INTO EIGHT SECTIONS.

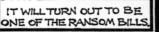

IT WILL TURN OUT TO BE ONE OF THE RANSOM BILLS.

THE CASHIER CLEARLY REMEMBERS THE MAN'S FACE...

HIGH CHEEKBONES, FLAT CHEEKS, POINTED CHIN, AND VACANT BLUE EYES.

WELL INTO THE YEAR 1934, THE RANSOM MONEY—OFTEN AS MUCH AS $40 PER WEEK—CONTINUES TO APPEAR. NONE OF THE BILLS THUS FAR CAN BE TRACED TO ITS SOURCE.

SATURDAY, SEPTEMBER 15, 1934
THE BREAK COMES AT LAST...

NA OIL CO

AT A FILLING STATION AT 127TH ST. AND LEXINGTON AVE. IN UPPER MANHATTAN.

A MAN IN A BLUE DODGE PAYS FOR HIS GAS WITH A $10 GOLD CERTIFICATE.

SUSPICIOUS OF THE BILL, THE ATTENDANT RECORDS THE LICENSE NUMBER OF THE CAR AS IT LEAVES THE STATION.

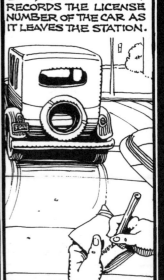

PART FIVE
THE ACCUSED

WEDNESDAY, SEPTEMBER 19, 1934
NEW YORK POLICE HAVE TRACED THE OWNER OF THE CAR TO A HOUSE AT 1279 E. 222ND STREET IN THE BRONX.

THE UPPER FLOOR IS THE HOME OF RICHARD HAUPTMANN, AGE 35, A CARPENTER BY TRADE.

OFFICERS SURROUND THE HOUSE IN THE EARLY MORNING, WATCHING FOR ANY MOVEMENT.

AT ABOUT 8:15 AM, A MAN EMERGES.

INSTEAD OF ARRESTING HIM ON THE SPOT, POLICE WATCH AS HE WALKS TO A GARAGE ACROSS THE ALLEY.

AND DRIVES OFF IN THE BLUE DODGE.

THE MAN IS STOPPED AS HE DRIVES DOWN PARK AVENUE IN THE FORDHAM SECTION OF THE BRONX.

WHAT IS THIS?

A SEARCH OF HIS PERSON YIELDS A $20 GOLD CERTIFICATE, FOLDED INTO EIGHT SECTIONS.

IT WILL TURN OUT TO BE ONE OF THE RANSOM BILLS.

POLICE BRING HAUPTMANN BACK TO HIS SECOND-FLOOR APARTMENT.

THERE, HE REJOINS HIS WIFE, ANNA, AND THEIR 1-YEAR-OLD SON MANFRED.

THE TWO UNDERGO AN EXTENSIVE QUESTIONING AS OFFICERS SEARCH THE APARTMENT THOROUGHLY.

AMONG THE ITEMS FOUND: A PAIR OF HIGH-POWERED BINOCULARS, AN ASSORTMENT OF STATE ROAD-MAPS, A HUNTING RIFLE, 17 MEMORANDUM BOOKS, WRITTEN IN GERMAN...

AND A STACK OF RAW SEAL-SKINS (THE MAN EXPLAINS THAT, AS A A SIDE-LINE, HE BUYS AND SELLS FURS).

IN THE AFTERNOON, HAUPTMANN IS BROUGHT DOWNTOWN TO THE NYPD'S 2ND PRECINCT STATION AT 130 GREENWICH STREET FOR A THOROUGH INTERROGATION.

THIS WILL INCLUDE A CERTAIN AMOUNT OF PHYSICAL "PERSUASION."

NEVERTHELESS, THE MAN FORCEFULLY DENIES HAVING HAD ANY PART IN EITHER THE KIDNAPPING OR THE EXTORTION OF THE RANSOM MONEY.

HIS FULL NAME IS:
BRUNO RICHARD HAUPTMANN.

HE IS AN IMMIGRANT FROM GERMANY AND SPEAKS WITH A HEAVY ACCENT.

HE PREFERS TO BE CALLED RICHARD OR DICK.

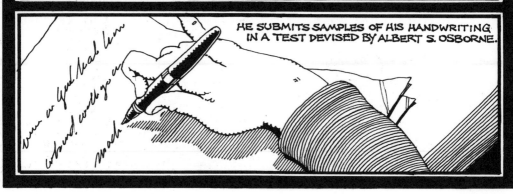

HE SUBMITS SAMPLES OF HIS HANDWRITING IN A TEST DEVISED BY ALBERT S. OSBORNE.

HAUPTMANN, STANDING AMONG BURLY POLICEMEN, IS PRESENTED IN A "LINE-UP."

AMONG THOSE CALLED TO IDENTIFY HIM ARE...

CAB DRIVER JOSEPH PERRONE, WHO DELIVERED THE KIDNAPPER'S NOTE TO THE CONDON HOME ON MARCH 12, 1932.

CECILE M. BARR, THEATRE CASHIER, WHO RECEIVED THE FOLDED RANSOM BILL ON NOVEMBER 26, 1933.

THE SERVICE STATION ATTENDANT WHO COPIED HAUPTMANN'S LICENSE PLATE NUMBER ON SEPTEMBER 15, 1934.

AND, MOST CRUCIALLY, DR. JOHN F. CONDON.

ALL PICK HAUPTMANN READILY ENOUGH EXCEPT FOR THE EVER-ECCENTRIC CONDON. HE FEELS HE NEEDS MORE TIME.

HE SLOWLY SCRUTINIZES EACH MAN, THEN TALKS PRIVATELY WITH HAUPTMANN, INCLUDING A FEW SENTENCES OF GERMAN.

HE ASKS THE PRISONER TO READ SEVERAL PHRASES ALOUD.

IT IS TOO DANGEROUS!

HE WOULD SMACK ME UP!

TO THE EXASPERATION OF POLICE, CONDON REFUSES TO IDENTIFY THE MAN AT THIS PARTICULAR PLACE AND TIME.

HIS ROUNDABOUT PLOY, HE WILL LATER CLAIM, IS TO CONVINCE HAUPTMANN TO CONFESS HIS CRIME.

THURSDAY, SEPTEMBER 20
AT THE HAUPTMANN RESIDENCE, THE SEARCHERS HAVE BY NOW SHIFTED THEIR ATTENTION TO THE RAMSHACKLE WOODEN GARAGE ACROSS THE ALLEY.

INSIDE, THERE IS A CARPENTER'S WORK-BENCH.

THE TOOL SET IS MISSING A THREE-QUARTER-INCH CHISEL, THE SAME SIZE AS WAS FOUND AT THE LINDBERGH HOUSE.

BEHIND A BOARD NAILED ACROSS TWO UPRIGHTS ARE FOUND TWO PACKAGES OF $10 GOLD CERTIFICATES, ABOUT $1830, ALL OF THEM RANSOM BILLS.

ANOTHER BUNDLE OF BILLS IS FOUND IN A 1-GALLON SHELLAC CAN: TWELVE PACKAGES, ADDING UP TO $11,960.

OVER THE NEXT SEVERAL DAYS, THE GARAGE WILL BE SLOWLY DISMANTLED.

A FURTHER $840 WILL BE FOUND, FOR A TOTAL OF $14,600 — A MERE FRACTION OF THE FULL RANSOM PAYMENT.

HE HAS GIVEN THE POLICE HIS ALIBIS FOR THREE IMPORTANT DATES...

ON TUESDAY, MARCH 1, 1932, THE DAY OF THE KIDNAPPING, HE WAS IN MANHATTAN, SEARCHING FOR WORK AT VARIOUS BUILDING SITES.

AT 7:00 PM, HE MET HIS WIFE AT HER PLACE OF EMPLOYMENT, FREDERICK'S BAKERY IN THE BRONX.

THEY ATE DINNER THERE AND THEN WENT HOME TO BED.

ON SATURDAY, APRIL 2, 1932, THE NIGHT OF THE RANSOM PAYMENT, HE WAS AT HOME ENJOYING A MUSICAL EVENING WITH HIS FRIEND HANS KLOPPENBURG.

THEY GET TOGETHER ON THE FIRST SATURDAY OF EVERY MONTH TO PLAY AND SING THEIR FAVORITE GERMAN SONGS.

SUNDAY, NOVEMBER 26, 1933, THE NIGHT THE MYSTERIOUS PATRON TOSSED THE FOLDED BILL TO THE THEATRE CASHIER, HAPPENED TO HAVE BEEN HAUPTMANN'S BIRTHDAY.

HE CELEBRATED AT HOME WITH HIS WIFE AND A FEW FRIENDS.

HOW DID HAUPTMANN SUPPORT HIS FAMILY, HE IS ASKED, SINCE HE QUIT HIS JOB, IN APRIL OF 1932, AT THE MAJESTIC APARTMENTS IN MANHATTAN?

HOW DID HE AFFORD SUCH RECENT INDULGENCES AS A NEW VICTROLA AND A TRIP TO GERMANY FOR HIS WIFE?

THE PRISONER EXPLAINS THAT HE BEGAN TO INVEST IN THE STOCK MARKET AROUND THAT TIME...

AND HAD DONE SO WELL THAT THE FAMILY COULD LIVE DECENTLY ON THE EARNINGS.

HOW DID HAUPTMANN COME INTO POSSESSION OF SO MUCH OF THE LINDBERGH RANSOM MONEY?

FISCH

HE SAYS THAT HE FOUND IT AMONG SEVERAL BOXES OF PERSONAL ITEMS LEFT TO HIM BY HIS FRIEND AND BUSINESS PARTNER ISADOR FISCH.

HE AND FISCH ENGAGED IN SEVERAL VENTURES TOGETHER, INCLUDING THE FUR-IMPORTING ENTERPRISE.

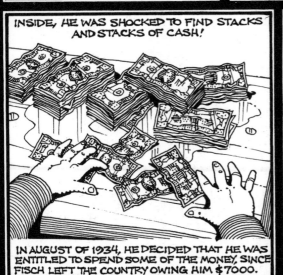

BUT FISCH, SUFFERING FROM TUBERCULOSIS, RETURNED TO GERMANY IN DECEMBER OF 1933, AND DIED IN LIEPZIG ON MARCH 29, 1934.

ONE OF THE BOXES WAS STORED BY HAUPTMANN ON THE TOP SHELF OF A KITCHEN CLOSET...

UNTIL ONE DAY, DURING A HEAVY RAIN, A LEAK IN THE ROOF SOAKED THE CONTAINER.

INSIDE, HE WAS SHOCKED TO FIND STACKS AND STACKS OF CASH!

IN AUGUST OF 1934, HE DECIDED THAT HE WAS ENTITLED TO SPEND SOME OF THE MONEY, SINCE FISCH LEFT THE COUNTRY OWING HIM $7000.

DESPITE HIS DENIALS, THE PRISONER IS CHARGED THIS AFTERNOON WITH EXTORTION.

BUT COL. SCHWARZKOPF BELIEVES THAT THE STATE OF NEW JERSEY WILL BE ABLE TO NAB HIM FOR THE GREATER CRIME.

AS HAUPTMANN'S PAST LIFE IN GERMANY IS SLOWLY UNCOVERED, IT REFLECTS UPON HIM POORLY.

HE HAS TOLD POLICE THAT HIS RECORD IS CLEAN, BUT IT TURNS OUT HE WAS CONVICTED SEVERAL TIMES OF LARCENY, ROBBERY AND BURGLARY.

HE ESCAPED FROM JAIL SEVERAL TIMES...

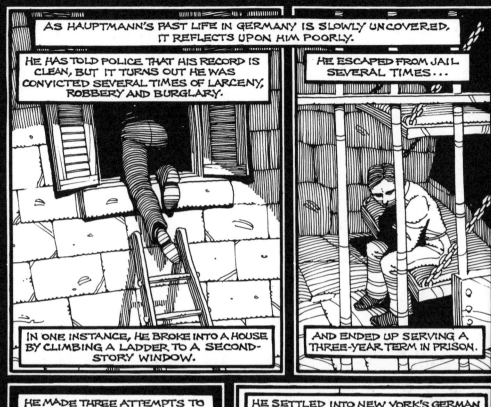

IN ONE INSTANCE, HE BROKE INTO A HOUSE BY CLIMBING A LADDER TO A SECOND-STORY WINDOW.

AND ENDED UP SERVING A THREE-YEAR TERM IN PRISON.

HE MADE THREE ATTEMPTS TO FLEE TO AMERICA, FINALLY MAKING IT —AS A STOWAWAY— IN 1923.

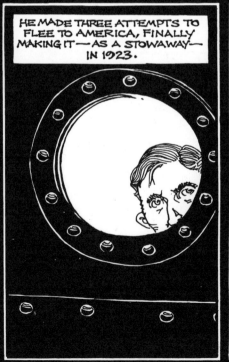

HE SETTLED INTO NEW YORK'S GERMAN COMMUNITY AND HAS SINCE LIVED A SEEMINGLY ORDINARY LIFE.

ON OCTOBER 10, 1925, HE MARRIED ANNA SCHOEFFLER, AN IMMIGRANT LIKE HIMSELF. IN 1933, THEIR SON MANFRED WAS BORN.

MONDAY, SEPTEMBER 24 OFFICERS STILL SEARCHING THE HAUPTMANN HOME COME ACROSS A NEW PIECE OF EVIDENCE.

THE ADDRESS AND TELEPHONE NUMBER OF JOHN F. CONDON ARE FOUND WRITTEN IN PENCIL ON THE DOOR FRAME INSIDE A BEDROOM CLOSET; ALSO THE SERIAL NUMBERS OF TWO OF THE RANSOM BILLS.

HAUPTMANN RESPONDS THAT HE DOESN'T RECALL HAVING WRITTEN THE NUMBERS... BUT HE MIGHT HAVE, SINCE HE WAS FOLLOWING THE CASE AT THE TIME.

NYC POLICE 128221 9 21 34

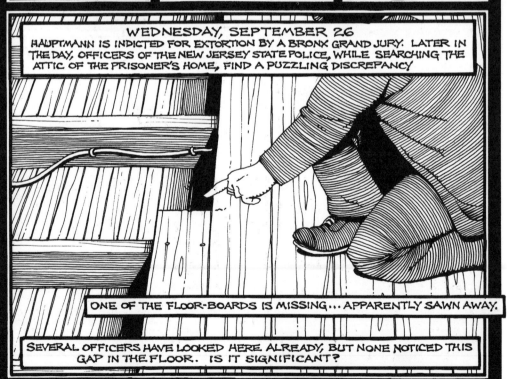

WEDNESDAY, SEPTEMBER 26
HAUPTMANN IS INDICTED FOR EXTORTION BY A BRONX GRAND JURY. LATER IN THE DAY, OFFICERS OF THE NEW JERSEY STATE POLICE, WHILE SEARCHING THE ATTIC OF THE PRISONER'S HOME, FIND A PUZZLING DISCREPANCY

ONE OF THE FLOOR-BOARDS IS MISSING... APPARENTLY SAWN AWAY.

SEVERAL OFFICERS HAVE LOOKED HERE ALREADY, BUT NONE NOTICED THIS GAP IN THE FLOOR. IS IT SIGNIFICANT?

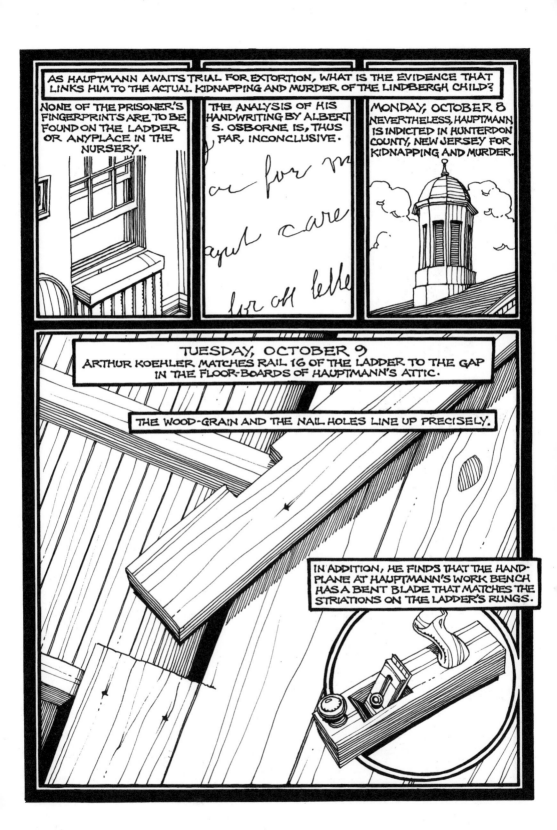

AS HAUPTMANN AWAITS TRIAL FOR EXTORTION, WHAT IS THE EVIDENCE THAT LINKS HIM TO THE ACTUAL KIDNAPPING AND MURDER OF THE LINDBERGH CHILD?

NONE OF THE PRISONER'S FINGERPRINTS ARE TO BE FOUND ON THE LADDER OR ANYPLACE IN THE NURSERY.

THE ANALYSIS OF HIS HANDWRITING BY ALBERT S. OSBORNE IS, THUS FAR, INCONCLUSIVE.

MONDAY, OCTOBER 8 NEVERTHELESS, HAUPTMANN IS INDICTED IN HUNTERDON COUNTY, NEW JERSEY FOR KIDNAPPING AND MURDER.

TUESDAY, OCTOBER 9 ARTHUR KOEHLER MATCHES RAIL 16 OF THE LADDER TO THE GAP IN THE FLOOR-BOARDS OF HAUPTMANN'S ATTIC.

THE WOOD-GRAIN AND THE NAIL HOLES LINE UP PRECISELY.

IN ADDITION, HE FINDS THAT THE HAND-PLANE AT HAUPTMANN'S WORK BENCH HAS A BENT BLADE THAT MATCHES THE STRIATIONS ON THE LADDER'S RUNGS.

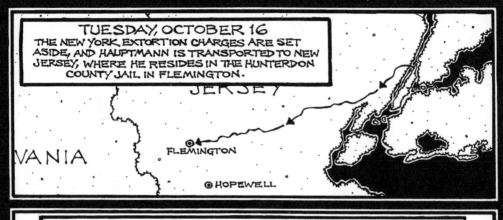

TUESDAY, OCTOBER 16
THE NEW YORK EXTORTION CHARGES ARE SET ASIDE, AND HAUPTMANN IS TRANSPORTED TO NEW JERSEY, WHERE HE RESIDES IN THE HUNTERDON COUNTY JAIL IN FLEMINGTON.

JERSEY

VANIA

◎ FLEMINGTON

◎ HOPEWELL

FRIDAY, NOVEMBER 2
HE ACQUIRES A HIGH-PROFILE DEFENCE ATTORNEY IN THE PERSON OF THE FLAMBOYANT VETERAN EDWARD J. REILLY OF BROOKLYN...

WHOSE SERVICES ARE PAID FOR BY WILLIAM RANDOLPH HEARST'S NEW YORK JOURNAL—IN EXCHANGE FOR MRS. HAUPTMANN'S EXCLUSIVE STORY.

REILLY WILL BE ASSISTED BY THREE NEW YORK ATTORNEYS: C. LLOYD FISHER, FREDERICK A. POPE AND EGBERT ROSECRANS.

PART SIX
THE TRIAL OF THE CENTURY

WEDNESDAY, JANUARY 2, 1935
THE TRIAL OF BRUNO RICHARD HAUPTMANN OPENS AT THE
HUNTERDON COUNTY COURTHOUSE IN FLEMINGTON.

THE SMALL TOWN IS JAMMED WITH THE PRESS AND PUBLIC,
ITS SINGLE HOTEL FILLED BEYOND CAPACITY.

AMONG THE WELL-KNOWN JOURNALISTS IN ATTENDANCE: WALTER WINCHELL,
EDNA FERBER, DAMON RUNYON, FANNIE HURST, ALEXANDER WOOLCOTT.

ALMOST EVERYONE HAS ALREADY PRONOUNCED THE DEFENDANT GUILTY.

THE COURTROOM IS CALLED TO ORDER BY JUDGE THOMAS TRENCHARD.

THE PROSECUTION TEAM IS HEADED BY NEW JERSEY'S ATTORNEY GENERAL, DAVID T. WILENTZ.

THE FIRST DAY IS TAKEN UP BY THE SELECTION OF A JURY.

A PANEL OF EIGHT MEN AND FOUR WOMEN—SOLID CITIZENS ALL—IS AGREED UPON.

IN AN UNPRECEDENTED DECISION, NEWSREEL CAMERAS WILL BE ALLOWED TO RECORD CERTAIN PORTIONS OF THE PROCEEDINGS.

SINCE THERE WERE NO EYEWITNESSES TO THE CRIME, THE PROSECUTION PLANS TO INTRODUCE A MOUNTAIN OF CIRCUMSTANTIAL EVIDENCE.

WILENTZ PRESENTS HIS CASE IN TWO PHASES: THE FIRST IS TO ESTABLISH THAT HAUPTMANN HAD OBTAINED AND SPENT THE RANSOM MONEY.

AMONG THE FIRST TO TAKE THE WITNESS STAND IS CHARLES A. LINDBERGH HIMSELF.

HE INSISTS THAT IT WAS THE DEFENDANT'S VOICE HE HEARD FROM THE CEMETERY ON THE NIGHT THE RANSOM WAS PAID.

JOHN F. CONDON ENDURES TWO DAYS ON THE STAND.

HE CANNOT BE SHAKEN FROM HIS IDENTIFICATION OF HAUPTMANN AS THE MAN CALLING HIMSELF "JOHN," WITH WHOM HE TALKED PERSONALLY ON TWO SEPARATE OCCASIONS.

THE THEATRE CASHIER CECILE BARR...

ESTABLISHES THAT THE DEFENDANT WAS IN POSSESSION OF RANSOM BILLS LONG BEFORE HE CLAIMED TO HAVE RECOVERED THEM FROM HIS CLOSET.

THE CAB DRIVER JOSEPH PERRONE...

POINTS TO HAUPTMANN AS HAVING HANDED HIM AN ENVELOPE TO DELIVER TO THE CONDON HOME ON MARCH 12, 1932.

THE HANDWRITING CASE IS SECURED BY ALBERT S. OSBORNE AND SEVEN OTHER DOCUMENT EXPERTS.

ALL CONFIRM THAT HAUPTMANN ALONE WROTE THE KIDNAPPING NOTES.

THE PROSECUTION'S SECOND PHASE IS AN ATTEMPT TO PLACE HAUPTMANN IN THE VICINITY OF THE LINDBERGH HOUSE ON MARCH 1, 1933. THREE MEN TESTIFY AS TO HAVING SEEN HIM ON THAT DAY.

MILLARD WHITED AND AMANDUS HOCHMUTH, WHO LIVE NEAR THE LINDBERGH ESTATE...

AND CHARLES ROSSITER, A TRAVELLING SALESMAN WHO HAPPENED TO BE IN THE AREA.

THE RECOLLECTIONS OF ALL THREE ARE PUT INTO DOUBT BY THE DEFENSE. HOCHMUTH, IN FACT, IS NEARLY BLIND FROM CATARACTS.

THE FINAL WITNESS FOR THE STATE IS THE WOOD EXPERT ARTHUR KOEHLER. HE SHOWS THE JURY HOW RAIL 16 OF THE KIDNAP LADDER LINES UP WITH THE FLOOR-BOARD IN THE DEFENDANT'S ATTIC.

AND HE DEMONSTRATES HOW THE PLANE FROM HAUPTMANN'S WORK-BENCH MATCHES THE TOOL-MARKS ON THE LADDER'S RUNGS.

WITH THIS, THE PROSECUTION RESTS ITS CASE.

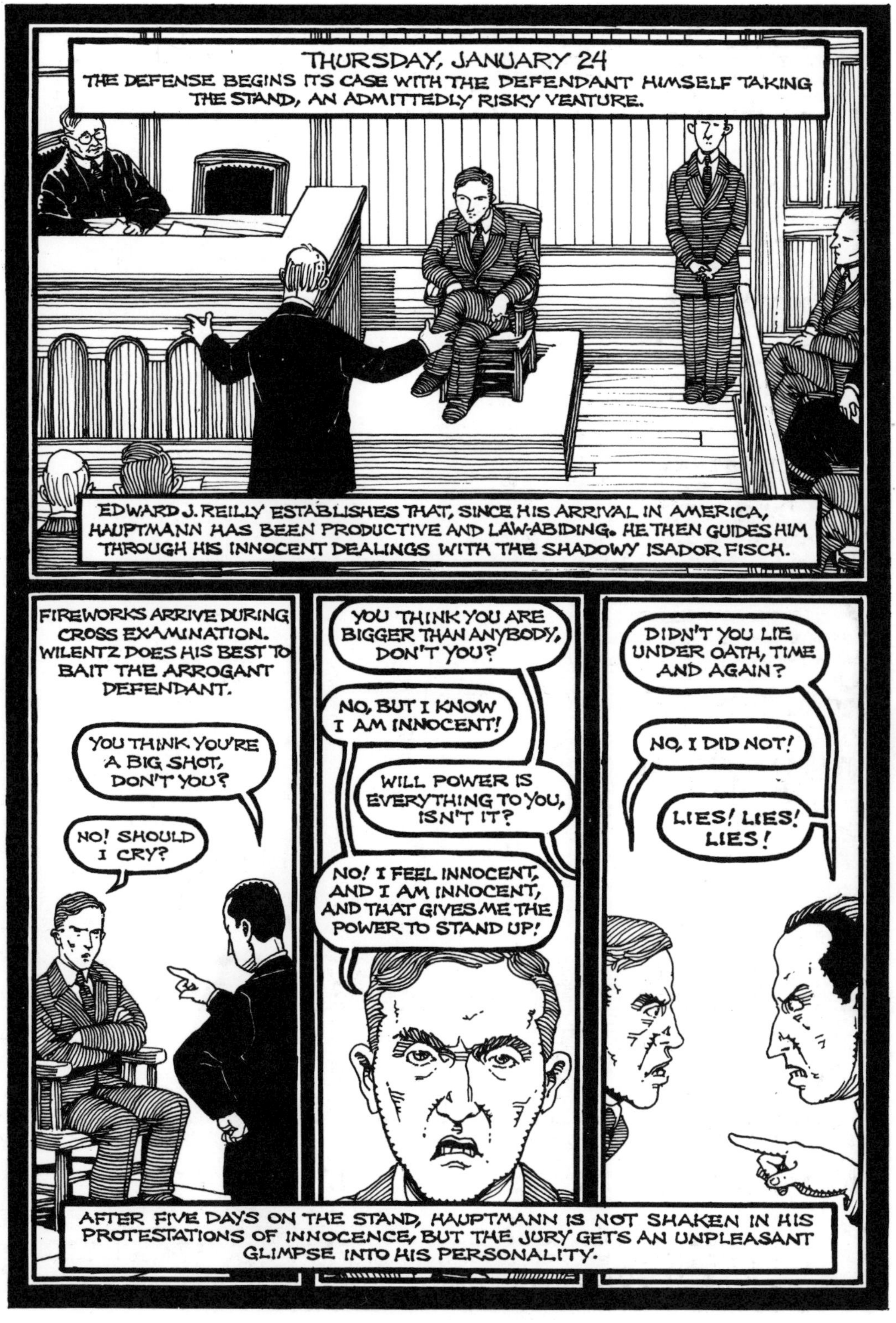
THURSDAY, JANUARY 24
THE DEFENSE BEGINS ITS CASE WITH THE DEFENDANT HIMSELF TAKING THE STAND, AN ADMITTEDLY RISKY VENTURE.
EDWARD J. REILLY ESTABLISHES THAT, SINCE HIS ARRIVAL IN AMERICA, HAUPTMANN HAS BEEN PRODUCTIVE AND LAW-ABIDING. HE THEN GUIDES HIM THROUGH HIS INNOCENT DEALINGS WITH THE SHADOWY ISADOR FISCH.
FIREWORKS ARRIVE DURING CROSS EXAMINATION. WILENTZ DOES HIS BEST TO BAIT THE ARROGANT DEFENDANT.
YOU THINK YOU'RE A BIG SHOT, DON'T YOU?
NO! SHOULD I CRY?
YOU THINK YOU ARE BIGGER THAN ANYBODY, DON'T YOU?
NO, BUT I KNOW I AM INNOCENT!
WILL POWER IS EVERYTHING TO YOU, ISN'T IT?
NO! I FEEL INNOCENT, AND I AM INNOCENT, AND THAT GIVES ME THE POWER TO STAND UP!
DIDN'T YOU LIE UNDER OATH, TIME AND AGAIN?
NO, I DID NOT!
LIES! LIES! LIES!
AFTER FIVE DAYS ON THE STAND, HAUPTMANN IS NOT SHAKEN IN HIS PROTESTATIONS OF INNOCENCE, BUT THE JURY GETS AN UNPLEASANT GLIMPSE INTO HIS PERSONALITY.

THE REMAINDER OF THE DEFENSE CASE CONSISTS OF SEVERAL DUBIOUS WITNESSES AND "EXPERTS."

THESE INCLUDE CHRISTIAN AND KATIE FREDERICKSON, PROPRIETORS OF FREDERICKSON'S BAKERY, AND CERTAIN OF THEIR CUSTOMERS, WHO CLAIM TO HAVE SEEN HAUPTMANN THERE ON THE EVENING OF MARCH 1, 1932.

TWO GENTLEMEN, BEN LUPICA AND WILLIAM BOLMER, WERE IN THE VICINITY OF THE LINDBERGH ESTATE ON THAT NIGHT.

THEY EACH DESCRIBE HAVING SEEN A MYSTERIOUS CAR, CONTAINING A MAKESHIFT-LOOKING LADDER, AND DRIVEN BY A MAN WHO LOOKED NOTHING LIKE THE DEFENDANT.

FRIENDS OF THE HAUPTMANNS, INCLUDING HANS KLOPPENBURG AND GRETA HENKEL TESTIFY AS TO THE DEFENDANT'S GOOD CHARACTER...

AND REPORT HAVING SEEN ISADOR FISCH IN HIS COMPANY UPON SEVERAL OCCASIONS.

THE DEFENSE CALLS ITS SINGLE HANDWRITING AUTHORITY IN THE PERSON OF JOHN TRENDLEY.

HE INSISTS THAT HAUPTMANN DID NOT WRITE THE RANSOM NOTES, DISPLAYING SEVERAL POINTS OF DISSIMILARITY.

LIKEWISE A LONE "WOOD EXPERT," CHARLES DE BISSCHOP, A LUMBERMAN, NURSERYMAN AND GENERAL CONTRACTOR.

HE MAINTAINS THAT RAIL 16 DOES NOT MATCH THE FLOOR-BOARD IN HAUPTMANN'S ATTIC.

MONDAY, FEBRUARY 11
EDWARD J. REILLY SUMS UP FOR THE DEFENSE.

THE CASE IS TOO PERFECT FROM THE PROSECUTION'S POINT OF VIEW. THERE ISN'T A MAN IN THE WORLD WITH BRAINS ENOUGH TO PLAN THIS KIDNAPPING ALONE, AND NOT WITH A GANG, AND THEN SIT DOWN AND MAKE THE FOOLISH MISTAKE OF RIPPING A BOARD OUT OF HIS ATTIC AND LEAVING THE OTHER HALF OF IT THERE.

I BELIEVE RICHARD HAUPTMANN IS ABSOLUTELY INNOCENT OF MURDER.

TUESDAY, FEBRUARY 12
DAVID WILENTZ, IN HIS SUMMATION FOR THE STATE, ABANDONS ANY PRETENSE OF THE VICTIM HAVING DIED ACCIDENTALLY.

WHAT TYPE OF MAN WOULD MURDER THE CHILD OF CHARLES AND ANNE LINDBERGH? HE WOULDN'T BE AN AMERICAN. NO AMERICAN GANGSTER EVER SANK TO THE LEVEL OF KILLING BABIES.

NO, IT HAD TO BE A FELLOW WHO HAD ICE WATER, NOT BLOOD, IN HIS VEINS. IT HAD TO BE A FELLOW WHO HAD A PECULIAR MENTAL MAKE-UP, WHO THOUGHT HE WAS BIGGER THAN LINDY. AN EGOMANIAC, WHO THOUGHT HE WAS OMNIPOTENT.

WEDNESDAY, FEBRUARY 13
THE TRIAL COMES TO AN END, AFTER 29 SESSIONS, 162 WITNESSES AND 381 EXHIBITS, AS THE JURY RETIRES TO CONSIDER ITS DECISION.

11½ HOURS LATER, THEY RETURN WITH THE NOT-UNEXPECTED VERDICT OF...

GUILTY.

WITH NO RECOMMENDATION OF MERCY — MEANING THAT THE JUDGE IS REQUIRED BY LAW TO SENTENCE THE DEFENDANT TO DEATH.

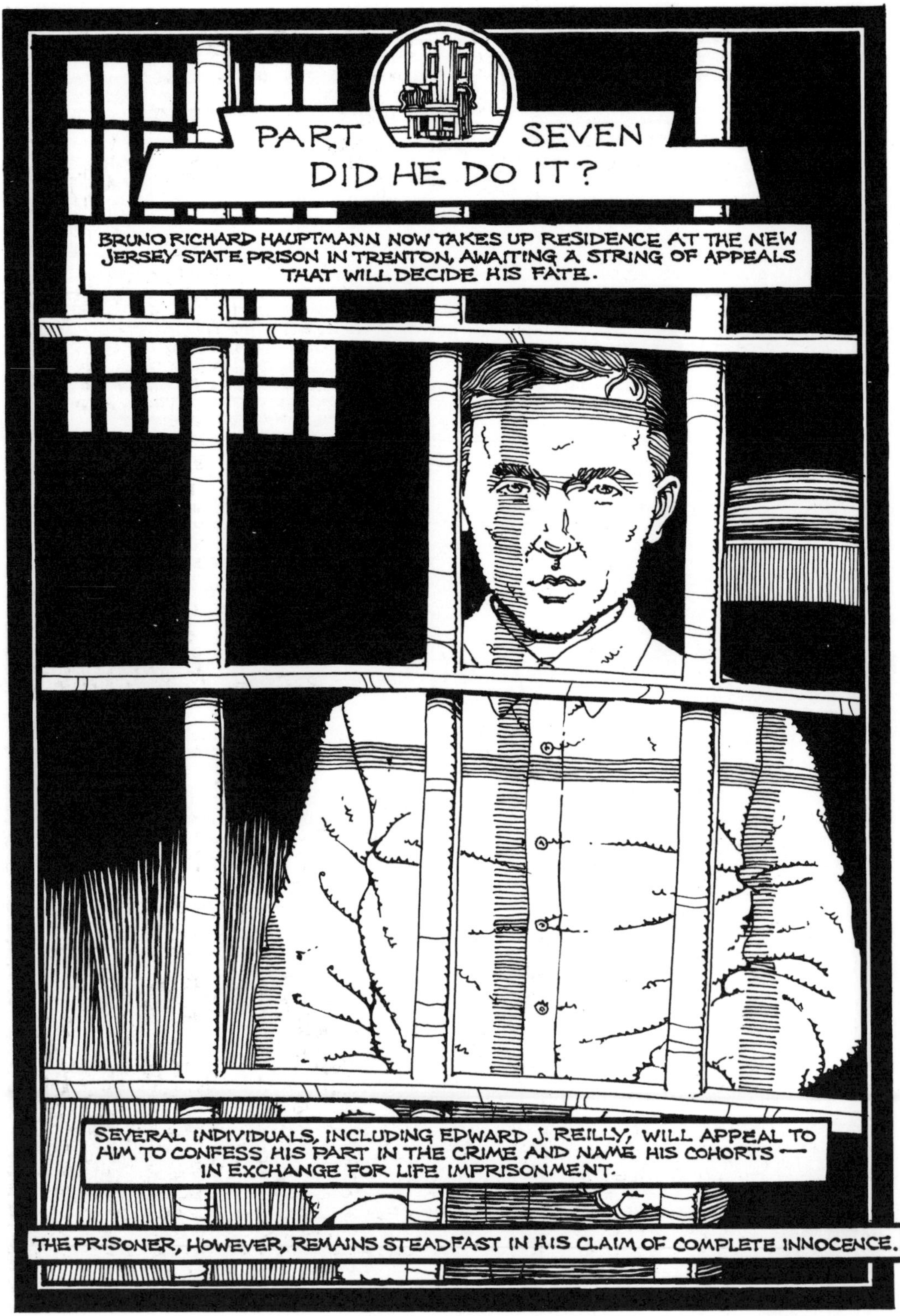
PART SEVEN
DID HE DO IT?
BRUNO RICHARD HAUPTMANN NOW TAKES UP RESIDENCE AT THE NEW JERSEY STATE PRISON IN TRENTON, AWAITING A STRING OF APPEALS THAT WILL DECIDE HIS FATE.
SEVERAL INDIVIDUALS, INCLUDING EDWARD J. REILLY, WILL APPEAL TO HIM TO CONFESS HIS PART IN THE CRIME AND NAME HIS COHORTS — IN EXCHANGE FOR LIFE IMPRISONMENT.
THE PRISONER, HOWEVER, REMAINS STEADFAST IN HIS CLAIM OF COMPLETE INNOCENCE.

OF THE DEFENSE TEAM, ONLY C. LLOYD FISHER REMAINS LOYAL TO THE CONVICTED MAN. HE PREPARES A BRIEF CITING INSTANCES OF PROSECUTORIAL MISCONDUCT.

DONE BY THE PROSECU...
AND HINDER THE DEFENSE.
1. DEFENSE WAS DENIED AN UP-TO-THE MINUTE COPY OF THE TRIAL TRANSCRIPT.
2. DEFENSE WAS NOT GIVEN ADEQUATE OPPORTUNITY TO EXAMINE THE RANSOM NOTES AND OTHER HANDWRITING EXHIBITS.
3. DEFENSE COUNSEL WAS DENIED PRIVATE CONFERENCE WITH THE DEFENDANT.
4. (a) DEFENSE WAS DENIED ACCESS TO THE HAUPTMANN HOME.
   (b) DEFENSE WAS DENIED ACCESS TO THE LINDBERGH HOUSE AND GROUNDS.
5. CROWDING THE PROSECUTION TABLE WITH ... INFLUENTIAL AND WELL-KNOWN ... THE STATE'S CASE

THE NEW JERSEY COURT OF APPEALS, HOWEVER, DENIES HIS PETITION, AND THE U.S. SUPREME COURT DECLINES TO REVIEW THE CASE.

HAUPTMANN'S CAUSE IS TAKEN UP BY NEW JERSEY'S NEW GOVERNOR, HAROLD HOFFMAN, WHO PUBLICLY STATES HIS BELIEF THAT THE LINDBERGH CASE IS STILL NOT SOLVED.

SUNDAY, JANUARY 12, 1936
HE GRANTS THE PRISONER A 30-DAY REPRIEVE AND ORDERS THE STATE POLICE TO RE-OPEN THE CASE.

ELLIS PARKER, SENIOR DETECTIVE OF BURLINGTON COUNTY, AND THE STATE'S MOST FAMOUS CRIME-BUSTER, SHARES THE GOVERNOR'S DOUBTS ABOUT HAUPTMANN'S GUILT.

PARKER'S THEORY IS THAT THE REMAINS FOUND IN THE WOODS WERE ERRONEOUSLY IDENTIFIED AND THAT THE LINDBERGH CHILD IS STILL ALIVE . . . .

AND IN THE HANDS OF THE ACTUAL KIDNAPPER, A DISBARRED TRENTON ATTORNEY AND EX-CONVICT NAMED PAUL H. WENDEL.

WEDNESDAY, FEBRUARY 13
PARKER AND A GROUP OF OTHERS ABDUCT WENDEL AND BEAT A CONFESSION OUT OF HIM.

BUT UPON HIS RELEASE SEVERAL WEEKS LATER, WENDEL RETRACTS THE CONFESSION, AND PARKER WILL LATER, IRONICALLY, BE TRIED FOR KIDNAPPING.

SPECULATION CONTINUES AMONG THE PUBLIC AND THE PRESS AS TO WHETHER HAUPTMANN WAS THE SOLE PERPETRATOR OF THE "CRIME OF THE CENTURY"... OR WAS HE PART OF A LARGER GANG — PERHAPS WITH THE AID OF SOMEONE WITHIN THE LINDBERGH HOUSEHOLD... OR IS HE AN INNOCENT MAN "FRAMED" BY THE AUTHORITIES?

THESE ARE THE IMPORTANT LINGERING QUESTIONS —

HOW WOULD HAUPTMANN HAVE KNOWN THAT THE LINDBERGHS HAD DECIDED TO LENGTHEN THEIR STAY AT THE HOPEWELL HOUSE THROUGH MARCH 1, 1932, INSTEAD OF RETURNING TO THE MORROW ESTATE, AS WAS THEIR ROUTINE?

MORE THAN HALF OF THE RANSOM PAYMENT HAS NEVER BEEN RECOVERED. COULD HAUPTMANN HAVE SPENT IT ALL? OR IS IT IN THE HANDS OF OTHERS? (AFTER HIS ARREST, THE BILLS STOPPED TURNING UP.)

ISADOR FISCH HAS PROVED TO BE A QUESTIONABLE CHARACTER WHO COULD VERY WELL HAVE BEEN IN THE BUSINESS OF "LAUNDERING" ILLEGALLY-OBTAINED CASH. DID HAUPTMANN RECEIVE THE MONEY QUITE INNOCENTLY AMONG THE POSSESSIONS HE LEFT BEHIND?

WHAT WAS THE ORIGIN OF THE "ITALIAN" VOICE HEARD IN THE BACKGROUND BY JOHN F. CONDON DURING HIS TELEPHONE CONVERSATION WITH "JOHN?" (ONE ANSWER: SINCE HAUPTMANN HAD NO TELEPHONE AT HIS HOME, HE MIGHT HAVE MADE THE CALL FROM AN ITALIAN RESTAURANT IN THE NEIGHBORHOOD.)

WHO WAS THE MYSTERIOUS "J. J. FAULKNER," WHO EXCHANGED $2980 OF RANSOM MONEY IN MAY OF 1933? THE HANDWRITING ON THE DEPOSIT SLIP HAS NEVER BEEN POSITIVELY LINKED TO HAUPTMANN.

WHO CONSTRUCTED THE KIDNAP LADDER? MANY HAVE DEEMED IT TOO PRIMITIVE AND SLAPDASH TO HAVE BEEN BUILT BY AN EXPERIENCED CARPENTER LIKE HAUPTMANN.

WHY WERE NONE OF HAUPTMANN'S FINGERPRINTS FOUND ON THE LADDER OR ANYPLACE IN THE NURSERY? INDEED, WHY WERE NO PRINTS FROM ANYBODY, SAVE THE CHILD HIMSELF, FOUND IN THE BABY'S ROOM?

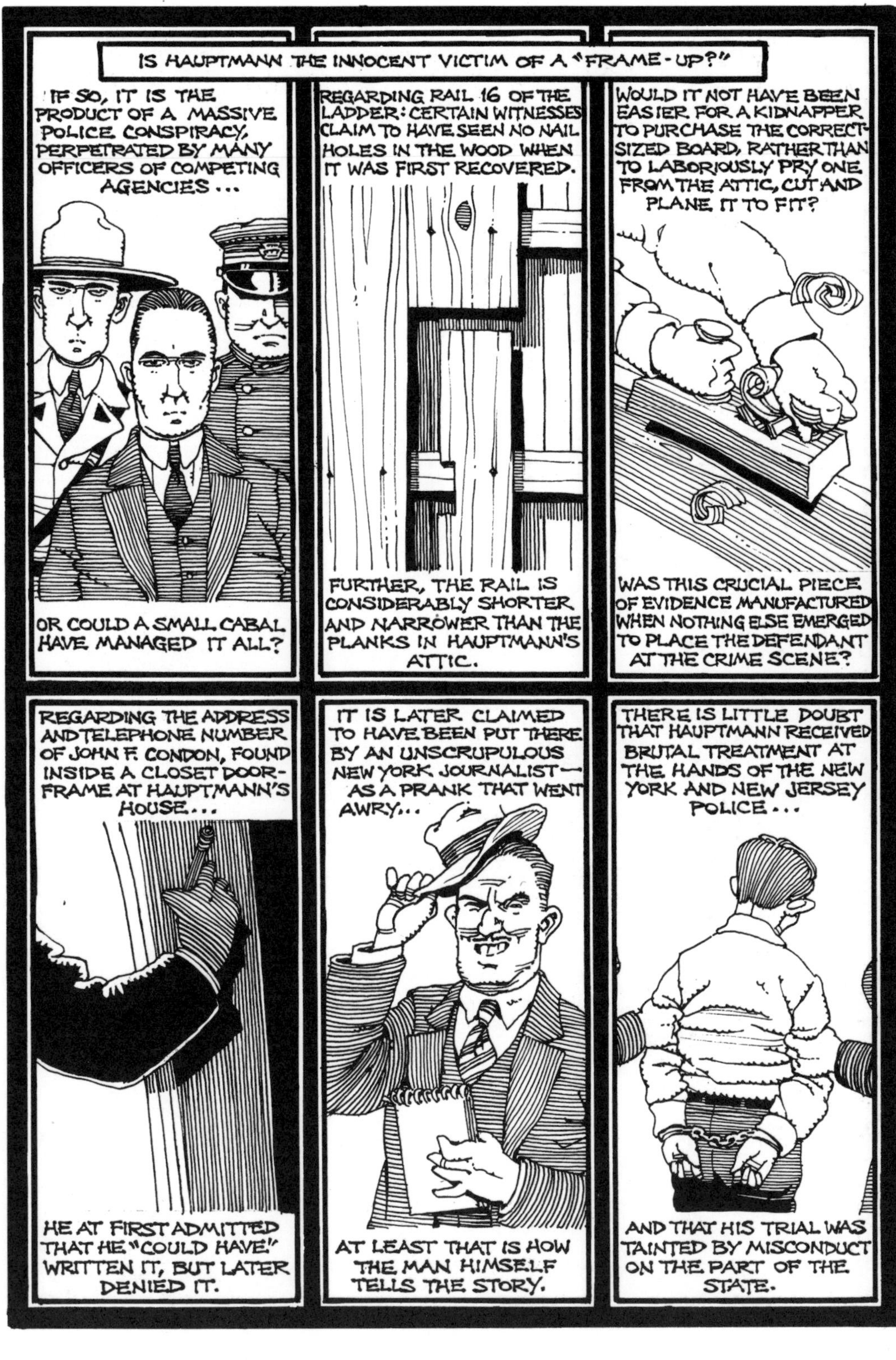
IS HAUPTMANN THE INNOCENT VICTIM OF A "FRAME-UP?"
IF SO, IT IS THE PRODUCT OF A MASSIVE POLICE CONSPIRACY, PERPETRATED BY MANY OFFICERS OF COMPETING AGENCIES...
OR COULD A SMALL CABAL HAVE MANAGED IT ALL?
REGARDING RAIL 16 OF THE LADDER: CERTAIN WITNESSES CLAIM TO HAVE SEEN NO NAIL HOLES IN THE WOOD WHEN IT WAS FIRST RECOVERED.
FURTHER, THE RAIL IS CONSIDERABLY SHORTER AND NARROWER THAN THE PLANKS IN HAUPTMANN'S ATTIC.
WOULD IT NOT HAVE BEEN EASIER FOR A KIDNAPPER TO PURCHASE THE CORRECT-SIZED BOARD, RATHER THAN TO LABORIOUSLY PRY ONE FROM THE ATTIC, CUT AND PLANE IT TO FIT?
WAS THIS CRUCIAL PIECE OF EVIDENCE MANUFACTURED WHEN NOTHING ELSE EMERGED TO PLACE THE DEFENDANT AT THE CRIME SCENE?
REGARDING THE ADDRESS AND TELEPHONE NUMBER OF JOHN F. CONDON, FOUND INSIDE A CLOSET DOOR-FRAME AT HAUPTMANN'S HOUSE...
HE AT FIRST ADMITTED THAT HE "COULD HAVE" WRITTEN IT, BUT LATER DENIED IT.
IT IS LATER CLAIMED TO HAVE BEEN PUT THERE BY AN UNSCRUPULOUS NEW YORK JOURNALIST— AS A PRANK THAT WENT AWRY...
AT LEAST THAT IS HOW THE MAN HIMSELF TELLS THE STORY.
THERE IS LITTLE DOUBT THAT HAUPTMANN RECEIVED BRUTAL TREATMENT AT THE HANDS OF THE NEW YORK AND NEW JERSEY POLICE...
AND THAT HIS TRIAL WAS TAINTED BY MISCONDUCT ON THE PART OF THE STATE.

IF HAUPTMANN DID NOT DO IT, WHO DID?

THE MOST PERSISTENT THEORY POINTS TO A GANG OF PROFESSIONAL CRIMINALS, WORKING WITH THE "INSIDE" HELP OF A MEMBER OF THE LINDBERGH OR MORROW HOUSEHOLD STAFF...

SUCH AS VIOLET SHARPE.... THE WHATELEYS... OR BETTY GOW, IN LEAGUE WITH HER NORWEGIAN SWEETHEART HENRY "RED" JOHNSEN.

IN THIS SCENARIO, THE LADDER IS PLACED AS MISDIRECTION...

AS THE KIDNAPPER IS SIMPLY HANDED THE SLEEPING CHILD BY THE INSIDE ACCOMPLICE.

LATER THEORIES WILL PROPOSE MORE UNLIKELY CULPRITS... SUCH AS COL. LINDBERGH HIMSELF!

THE AVIATOR DROPS THE CHILD ACCIDENTALLY DURING ONE OF THE PRACTICAL JOKES OF WHICH HE IS SAID TO BE FOND.

THE CHILD IS BURIED IN THE WOODS, AND THE ENTIRE KIDNAPPING STORY IS MANUFACTURED BY LINDBERGH AND BRECKINRIDGE...

WHO PLANT A LADDER NEAR THE HOUSE AND SCRAWL A "RANSOM" NOTE.

TO THEIR MINDS, WITH NO FURTHER WORD FROM AN ABDUCTOR, THE INCIDENT WOULD EVENTUALLY BLOW OVER.

BUT AN ENTERPRISING CRIMINAL SEES A COPY OF THE NOTE AND INITIATES AN EXTORTION SCHEME BY FORGING OTHERS IN THE SAME HANDWRITING.

A VARIATION OF THIS THEORY HAS THE CHILD KILLED — ACCIDENTALLY OR DELIBERATELY — BY ANNE LINDBERGH'S UNBALANCED OLDER SISTER ELISABETH.

NONE OF THESE SCENARIOS, HOWEVER, ACCOUNTS FOR THE LADDER: WHERE DID IT COME FROM?

OBVIOUSLY HOME-MADE, BUT NOBODY HAS EVER COME FORWARD CLAIMING TO HAVE BUILT IT.

IN ANY CASE, WHY WOULD THE PUBLICITY-SHY LINDBERGH CONCOCT A FICTION THAT WOULD BRING HIM MAXIMUM PUBLIC EXPOSURE?

LINDY BABY STOLEN

AN ADJUNCT TO THE THEORIES CITED ABOVE MAINTAINS THAT THE LINDBERGH CHILD IS ALIVE YET.

THE REMAINS WERE, AFTER ALL, TOO DECOMPOSED TO PERMIT POSITIVE IDENTIFICATION.

THEY WERE EITHER THOSE OF A BOY RUN AWAY FROM A NEARBY ORPHANS' ASYLUM...

OR AN ANONYMOUS CORPSE PLACED BY GANGSTERS TO TAKE THE "HEAT" OFF OF THEM.

BETTY GOW "IDENTIFIES" THE BODY BECAUSE SHE IS PART OF THE PLOT...

THE LONE EAGLE FROM HIS DESIRE TO END THE SEARCH AND CLOSE THE CASE.

THE CHILD COULD HAVE FALLEN INTO THE HANDS OF A "BABY BROKER"...

THE RANSOM MONEY USED TO SET THE BOY UP WITH A FAMILY FAR AWAY, WHERE HE WILL GROW TO MANHOOD WITH NO IDEA OF HIS ORIGIN.

AS HE STATES IN THE RANSOM NOTES, THE PLAN HAS BEEN IN THE WORKS FOR ONE YEAR.

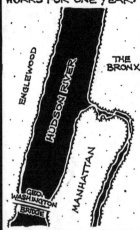

THAT TIME WAS SPENT SCRUTINIZING THE MORROW ESTATE IN ENGLEWOOD, JUST ACROSS THE HUDSON RIVER FROM THE BRONX.

HE GETS TO KNOW THE COMINGS AND GOINGS OF THE FAMILY.

THE 3-PART LADDER, WHEN EXTENDED TO ITS FULL LENGTH, REACHES TO THE SECOND-STORY WINDOW OF THE BABY'S NURSERY.

ON THE EVENING OF MARCH 1, 1932, HAVING HEARD THAT COL. LINDBERGH WILL BE IN NEW YORK ALL EVENING, HE DRIVES TO ENGLEWOOD...

FULLY INTENDING TO WAIT INTO THE NIGHT TO MAKE HIS MOVE.

ALONG THE WAY, HOWEVER, HE CATCHES A STRAY BIT OF GOSSIP, PERHAPS FROM AN EMPLOYEE OF THE HOUSE: THE LINDBERGHS ARE STILL AT HOPEWELL.

BUT NOW HE CANNOT BACK AWAY — HE HAS WORKED HIMSELF INTO A FEVER. TONIGHT HAS TO BE THE NIGHT!

SO HE DRIVES THE 50 MILES TO THE HOPEWELL ESTATE (WHICH HE HAS NO DOUBT VISITED BEFORE).

AND HERE HE SEIZES THE MOMENT.

DOES HE INTEND TO KILL THE CHILD? IF NOT, WHERE WOULD HE KEEP IT? NO ANSWER HAS YET ARISEN.

IN ANY CASE, THE MAN'S ARROGANCE WILL PREVENT HIM FROM EVER CONFESSING TO THE CRIME.

FRIDAY, APRIL 3, 1936
BRUNO RICHARD HAUPTMANN HAS AT LAST
EXHAUSTED HIS OPTIONS.

STILL PROCLAIMING HIS INNOCENCE, HE IS STRAPPED INTO
NEW JERSEY'S ELECTRIC CHAIR.
THE SWITCH IS PULLED AT 8:44 PM.

OVER THE YEARS, HAUPTMANN'S LOYAL WIDOW ANNA PROVES QUITE STEADFAST IN KEEPING HIS CAUSE ALIVE.

SHE TWICE SUES THE STATE OF NEW JERSEY: IN 1981 FOR HAVING WRONGFULLY EXECUTED HER HUSBAND, AND IN 1986 FOR HAVING FRAMED HIM FOR MURDER.

BOTH SUITS ARE DISMISSED. HER APPEAL TO THE U.S. SUPREME COURT IS LIKEWISE REJECTED.

ALSO OVER THE YEARS, AS MANY AS FIFTEEN INDIVIDUALS COME FORWARD CLAIMING TO BE THE "LINDBERGH BABY."

ONE OF THEM IS KENNETH KERWIN.

IN THE 1960s, HE CONFRONTS COL. LINDBERGH IN DARIEN, CONNECTICUT AND MUST BE TAKEN AWAY BY POLICE.

IN 1976, HE SUES THE LINDBERGH ESTATE FOR HIS RIGHTFUL INHERITANCE.

BUT HIS CLAIM, AND THOSE OF THE OTHERS, IS PROVED FALSE THROUGH FINGERPRINTS AND SIMPLE BLOOD TESTS.

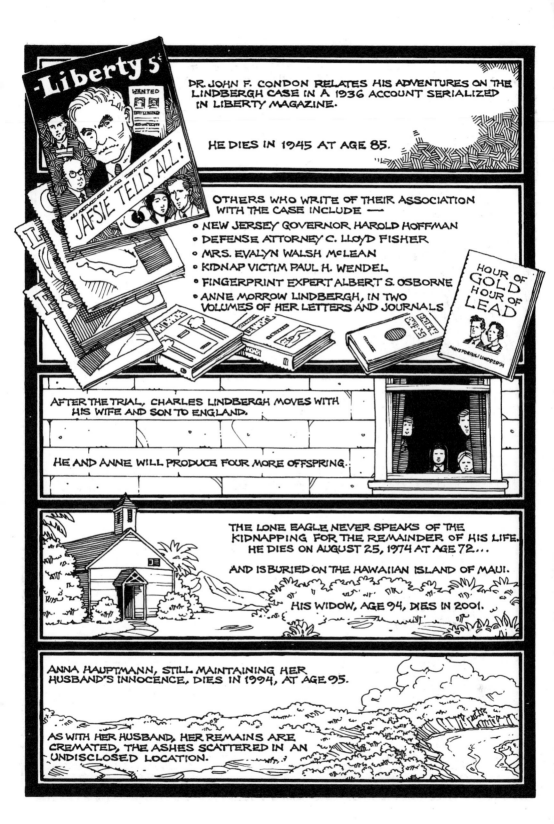

DR. JOHN F. CONDON RELATES HIS ADVENTURES ON THE LINDBERGH CASE IN A 1936 ACCOUNT SERIALIZED IN LIBERTY MAGAZINE.

HE DIES IN 1945 AT AGE 85.

OTHERS WHO WRITE OF THEIR ASSOCIATION WITH THE CASE INCLUDE —

• NEW JERSEY GOVERNOR HAROLD HOFFMAN
• DEFENSE ATTORNEY C. LLOYD FISHER
• MRS. EVALYN WALSH McLEAN
• KIDNAP VICTIM PAUL H. WENDEL
• FINGERPRINT EXPERT ALBERT S. OSBORNE
• ANNE MORROW LINDBERGH, IN TWO VOLUMES OF HER LETTERS AND JOURNALS

AFTER THE TRIAL, CHARLES LINDBERGH MOVES WITH HIS WIFE AND SON TO ENGLAND.

HE AND ANNE WILL PRODUCE FOUR MORE OFFSPRING.

THE LONE EAGLE NEVER SPEAKS OF THE KIDNAPPING FOR THE REMAINDER OF HIS LIFE. HE DIES ON AUGUST 25, 1974 AT AGE 72....

AND IS BURIED ON THE HAWAIIAN ISLAND OF MAUI.

HIS WIDOW, AGE 94, DIES IN 2001.

ANNA HAUPTMANN, STILL MAINTAINING HER HUSBAND'S INNOCENCE, DIES IN 1994, AT AGE 95.

AS WITH HER HUSBAND, HER REMAINS ARE CREMATED, THE ASHES SCATTERED IN AN UNDISCLOSED LOCATION.

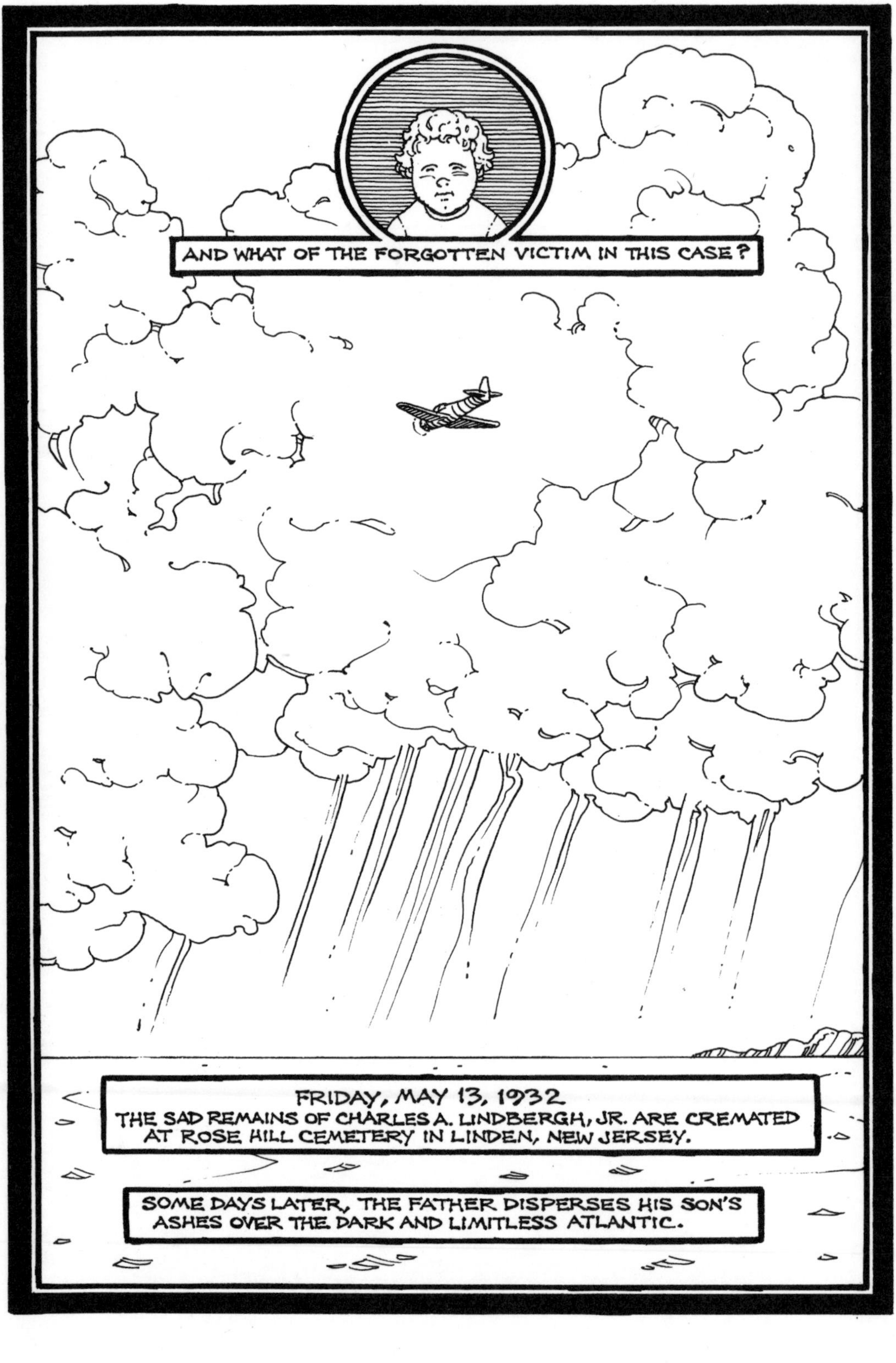
AND WHAT OF THE FORGOTTEN VICTIM IN THIS CASE?
FRIDAY, MAY 13, 1932
THE SAD REMAINS OF CHARLES A. LINDBERGH, JR. ARE CREMATED AT ROSE HILL CEMETERY IN LINDEN, NEW JERSEY.
SOME DAYS LATER, THE FATHER DISPERSES HIS SON'S ASHES OVER THE DARK AND LIMITLESS ATLANTIC.